EUROPEAN MONETARY UNION
AND
REGIONAL DEVELOPMENT

THE DAVID HUME INSTITUTE
FOR
BANK OF SCOTLAND

Hume Papers on Public Policy
Volume 5 No 1 Spring 1997

EUROPEAN MONETARY UNION

AND

REGIONAL DEVELOPMENT

Edited by
Gavin McCrone

EDINBURGH UNIVERSITY PRESS

© The David Hume Institute 1997

Edinburgh University Press
22 George Square, Edinburgh

Typeset in Times New Roman by WestKey Limited,
Falmouth, Cornwall and printed and bound in
Great Britain by Page Bros Limited, Norwich

A CIP record for this book is available from
the British Library.

ISBN 0 7486 0953 9

Contents

Contributors

Gavin McCrone is a professor in the Department of Business Studies, University of Edinburgh. From 1970 to 1992 he was Chief Economic Adviser to successive Secretaries of State for Scotland; he was also Secretary of the Industry Department for Scotland at The Scottish Office from 1980 to 1987 and of the Scottish Development Department from 1987 to 1992.

The Rt Hon Bruce Millan, PC, was European Commissioner for regional policy from 1989 until 1995. He was Secretary of State for Scotland from 1976 to 1979 and Minister of State at The Scottish Office from 1974 to 1976. Between 1966 and 1970 he held ministerial posts both at The Scottish Office and at the Ministry of Defence. He was Member of Parliament for Glasgow Craigton from 1959 to 1983 and for Glasgow Govan from 1983 until 1989.

Dr Norbert Walter has been Managing Director of Deutsche Bank Research since 1992, and Chief Economist of the Deutsche Bank Group since 1990. He has been a professor at the Kiel Institute for World Economics and John McCloy Distinguished Fellow at the American Institute for Contemporary German Studies in Washington. He joined Deutsche Bank in 1987.

Dr Carlo Santini has been Central Manager for Economic Research at the Bank of Italy since 1995. He joined the Bank of Italy in 1961 and has held various posts including head of the Balance of Payments Office, Manager of the International Sector, and head of the Foreign Department. From 1979 to 1980 he was seconded as economic adviser to the Italian Prime Minister.

Foreword

This book has its origins in a paper commissioned from Professor Gavin McCrone as background to the Bank of Scotland 1996 Colloquium, held in April of that year. Bank of Scotland provides in this way from time to time the opportunity for a few of its customers, friends and contacts, to reflect on broad political and social currents. Such pervasive issues affect the environment within which business transactions are completed day by day, but they also provide insights into the direction of future change for which successful businesses have to define strategies and tactics. The title for the 1996 Colloquium was 'Monetary Union and Regional Development'. After an excursion in 1994 into 'Corporate Governance and Capital Markets', we had returned to closer examination of some of the areas explored in 1992 under the general heading then of 'Prospects for Europe'.

Professor McCrone's original paper forms Part 1 of this book. Part 2 provides a report of the proceedings of the Colloquium. It embodies edited versions of the three keynote addresses presented by distinguished commentators. Each of them has very significant practical experience of dealing with the policy and business implications of the issues they were asked to explore. It is clear from the brief report of the stimulating discussion (under Chatham House rules) which followed each presentation that they provoked lively debate. We are very grateful indeed to former European Commissioner, the Right Honourable Bruce Millan, PC, to the Chief Economist of Deutsche Bank, Dr Norbert Walter, and to Dr Carlo Santini, the Central Manager for Economic Research at the Banca d'Italia, for the trouble they took to prepare and deliver their Colloquium papers, and for their patient courtesy reviewing the edited texts and agreeing to their publication. And we thank all the other distinguished participants who provided the lively discussion reported here. The final section of the book is again contributed by Professor McCrone, based on and developed from the overall summing up he offered at the close of the Colloquium. The months which have elapsed since then have seen further progress in defining the institutional framework under which EMU will be brought to life, and further debate and discussion about the importance, and meaning, of convergence of economic fundamentals. Reflections on these more recent developments are incorporated in this final section.

As this foreword is written – on the eve of the Dublin Summit – it seems clear that in the design for ERM Mark II there will be an institutional structure which Finance Ministers and Central Bank Governors of all Member States of the European Union believe will provide encouragement for those countries which do not join EMU as part of the initial core, and which will motivate them to align their individual monetary policies closely with those of the new European Central Bank. There is now more explicit acknowledgement of the importance of convergence of social as well as monetary policies. The need to work towards achieving flexibility in labour markets commensurate with the freedom of capital markets internationally and of the markets within the European Community for goods and services is discussed more openly. The potential risks of failure of a monetary union are acknowledged more explicitly, and drive a concern to ensure that its framework is robust, demanding, and rigorously disciplined.

But in all of this, the tensions of regional imbalances and the policies and instruments available within a European Monetary Union to address these and to modify their impact still receive scant attention. Competition among regions will actually be intensified by monetary union. Monetary union is not concerned with the re-distribution of the benefits of wealth creation but with optimising wealth creation untrammelled by the market distortions created by national, politically motivated, monetary policies. Bank of Scotland is a major UK bank rooted in a distinctive part of the political and monetary union of the United Kingdom. Scotland has both enjoyed and suffered from the consequences of regional economic differentiation. There is therefore for us and for many of our customers a particular interest in these and all other aspects of regional policy and development.

Our purpose in securing the publication of this book is to contribute to wider understanding of the implications of policies being considered and developed to secure greater economic and social stability throughout Europe. We hope that in doing so we have made some contribution to better informed public debate which will engage the attention of businessmen as well as politicians.

We are indebted many times over to Professor Gavin McCrone for this book. His work at the heart of economic policy as a senior civil servant in The Scottish Office, and his abiding interest in these issues as an academic, equip him uniquely to offer informed analysis and commentary.

We are indebted also to The David Hume Institute of Edinburgh for facilitating the publication of this book, and for bringing it to the attention of a wider audience than could be reached by the original small Colloquium from which it sprang.

Sir John Shaw, CBE
Deputy Governor
Bank of Scotland

November 1996

The David Hume Institute is pleased to have assisted in the wider dissemination of this valuable collection of papers on a topic of vital importance for the future of Scotland, the United Kingdom and the European Union. It is only necessary to add our thanks to Professor McCrone for his editorial work on this book, and to express our usual disclaimer to the effect that the views presented here are those of the authors and not those of either the Institute (which as a charity takes up no position on the matters discussed) or of Bank of Scotland.

Hector L MacQueen and Brian G M Main

Directors, The David Hume Institute

PART 1: THE ISSUES

Gavin McCrone

'So much of barbarism, however, still remains in the transactions of most civilised nations, that almost all independent countries choose to assert their nationality by having, to their own inconvenience and that of their neighbours, a peculiar currency of their own.'

John Stuart Mill

'Truth to tell, the notion of an economic and monetary union was closer to that of political union, federation or confederation, than to the notion of a customs union …All this would require profound changes for which the member countries were obviously not ready.'

Robert Marjolin
(Former Vice President of the Commission)

1   Introduction

Monetary union is not a new experience for Britain, or for Scotland. The Union of 1707 brought full monetary union between England and Scotland, when the pound Scots was replaced with sterling; and in 1826 a similar union took place between Great Britain and Ireland. These unions were a long time ago, but they had features which may still be of relevance today. The Scottish/English union was undertaken for reasons that were very similar to those which led to the original formation of the European Community. It was far from popular at the time, either in economic or political terms, and had there been a referendum, there would surely have been a large majority against it; but it may fairly be said to have laid the basis for Scotland's subsequent growth and prosperity.[1] The Irish union, on the other hand, is often judged by economic historians as having severely damaged Ireland's growth prospects in the first half of the nineteenth century.[2]

Both countries at the time of these unions were much poorer than England. The Scottish union followed the Darien disaster, in which a large part of Scotland's accumulated wealth was lost; perhaps in consequence of this the rate of 12 Scots pounds to one pound sterling, at which the union took place, did not over-value the Scots currency and appears to have enabled the Scottish economy to be competitive. There was also a substantial financial transfer from England to Scotland, known as the 'Equivalent', to enable Scotland's high outstanding debt to be reduced, thereby assisting 'convergence' (and perhaps having its present day parallel in the Cohesion Fund). The Irish monetary union followed the political union of 1800, and the currency, which had been fluctuating and had fallen to 25% less than sterling, was exchanged at par. This necessitated a severe deflation in Ireland both in the years up to 1826 and subsequently, which, it is claimed, caused the loss of many

---

[1]   Cameron, A (1995), *Bank of Scotland 1695–1995*, Edinburgh: Mainstream, pp 31–49.

[2]   Lynch, P, and J Vaizey (1960), *Guinness's Brewery in the Irish Economy 1759–1876*, Cambridge University Press, pp 32–36.

businesses.[3] The lesson to be drawn is that in any monetary union it is essential for the values at which the old currency is exchanged to reflect accurately the underlying economic strength of the participating economies, if one or other partner is not to suffer when the single currency is introduced.

There was another difference, though one not appreciated at the time. Scotland, like England, had many of the raw materials and energy resources which formed the basis of nineteenth-century industrialisation; Ireland did not. Even had Ireland achieved more industrial growth in the nineteenth century, it would have lacked much of the heavy industry that was typical of Britain's nineteenth-century prosperity. In the modern jargon Ireland and Britain were not, at least at that time, an 'optimum currency area'.[4]

There have been other much more recent quasi-monetary unions. The most important of these, the Gold Standard, lasted throughout much of the nineteenth century and up to 1914. It was centred on London and, apart from Britain and its extensive overseas dependencies, included the United States and much of Europe.[5] It therefore covered a large proportion of the trading world. There was a common reserve currency, gold, in which national currencies were fixed, without even the luxury of fluctuation margins as in the European Monetary System's exchange rate mechanism (ERM); and there was an anchor currency, sterling, which was widely used also as a substitute reserve currency. The system was managed by the Bank of England, and monetary policy was, in effect, taken out of the hands of participating countries. Moreover, although there was no formal economic union, and certainly not political union, United Kingdom trade was tariff free. This system formed the basis of a remarkable stability in the world monetary system and a substantial growth in trade. And although it did not provide for, nor depend upon, large inter-Government financial transfers of the kind sometimes argued for in the proposals for European Economic and Monetary Union (EMU), there were very large flows of private investment capital, mainly from Britain but also from France, to other countries.

The Bretton Woods system, which lasted from the end of the Second World War until 1971, was also a quasi-monetary union,

[3]   Ibidem.
[4]   Mundell, R A, (1963), 'Optimum Currency Areas', 51(4) *American Economic Review*.
[5]   Panic, M, (1992), *European Monetary Union: Lessons from the Classical Gold Standard*, London: Macmillan.

though a weaker one than the Gold Standard.[6] It became, in effect, a dollar exchange standard, with participating currencies quoted in values against the dollar and with the dollar fixed to gold. There were fluctuation values of 1% (compared with zero under the Gold Standard and 2.25% under the ERM currency grid before 1993). The system was managed by the United States and the dollar was the anchor currency. The par values of national currencies were occasionally altered in relation to the dollar, but for nearly twenty years there was remarkable stability: following the 1949 devaluation and general realignment the pound remained at $2.80 until 1967, when it was reduced to $2.40. The system therefore provided considerable stability; and while it lasted there were high rates of economic growth and low levels of unemployment, which have not been equalled since. It would seem, however, to be the experience of both the Gold Standard and Bretton Woods that the anchor currency tends to become overvalued; and, perhaps partly in consequence, that a substantial proportion of savings from the country managing the anchor currency get channelled into investment in other participating countries.[7] This tendency to overvaluation appears also to be a feature of the Deutschmark since it became the anchor of the ERM.

The present scheme for EMU should be seen against this background, but it differs from these previous unions in some important respects. Unlike the Gold Standard or Bretton Woods it involves not simply a common reserve currency, with fixed or pegged exchange rates for national currencies linked to it, but the eventual replacement of national currencies altogether by a single currency. In this respect it is similar to the Scottish/English and the Irish/Great Britain unions, but unlike them it does not involve political or fiscal union. The EMU scheme therefore breaks new ground: except in the case of Ireland/UK from 1922 to 1979 (from Ireland's independence to its membership of the ERM, when the link with sterling was broken) and the Belgium/Luxembourg union, both of which are rather special cases, a full monetary union involving a single currency has not been tried before without political and fiscal union. The question in the minds of some commentators, ranging from those who want to see

[6] Triffen, R, (1957), *Europe and the Money Muddle*, London: Oxford University Press; and idem, (1961), *Gold and the Dollar Crisis*, New Haven: Yale University Press.
[7] Panic (1992), op cit, and Triffen, R, in Baldasarri, M, and R Mundell (eds), (1993), *Building a New Europe*, London: Macmillan.

more integration at one extreme to the British Eurosceptics at the other, is whether this is feasible. Will the union fail for lack of the cohesion in economic management that political union would bring, or will it in the end compel political union against the wishes of those who continue to champion the nation state?

The proposals should be seen as a development of the earlier steps towards European economic integration. But EMU differs from the previous steps, the Treaty of Paris (which founded the Coal and Steel Community), the Treaty of Rome (which established the European Economic Community) and the Single European Act (which aimed to turn the customs union into a single market). This is not because it involves transfer of responsibility for economic policy (the others have involved that too) but because it carries substantial risk. The dismantling of tariffs and non-tariff barriers, required by earlier treaties, was not risk free. But the process was gradual, and it always remained open to countries to ensure the competitive position of their economies by exchange rate adjustment. Monetary union in its final stage, when a single currency replaces national currencies, will not only be accompanied by massive technical problems, but will leave Governments with substantially less power to adjust the competitive position of their economies.

But there is a risk either way. Obviously if EMU is embarked upon and fails, or if it is perceived subsequently by some participating countries not to have worked in their interest, the cause of European integration would receive a severe setback: even if this did not seriously damage the European Union, it could at least destroy its momentum for a long time to come. But it is less well appreciated, particularly in Britain, that there is also a major risk if it does not proceed. The Single Market programme, which included the lifting of controls on capital movements, has made the ERM regime of adjustable but pegged exchange rates within narrow bands, which operated with comparative success in the 1980s, impossible to sustain. Events have now shown that a return to the ERM, as it worked during the last decade, is unlikely to be possible. But it was this system which provided the stability that enabled further steps in the process of European union to be taken. Now that it is greatly weakened, if not destroyed, the comparative certainty over the terms on which trade can be conducted is lost; and there must be serious doubt that the Single Market can be properly achieved and maintained without the secure foundation of a stable monetary regime.

There is also a risk if EMU goes ahead only partially, with some of the present fifteen EU states. At the time of writing, this seems to be the most likely outcome. It would split the EU, unless there was either a clear expectation that the union will quickly spread to all members or some alternative regime is arranged to link the outsiders with the core, and it would still leave the problem of how monetary stability throughout the whole EU is to be achieved. This could have far reaching implications – not least for the United Kingdom – and the potential loss of influence and the consequences of failure to achieve the full benefits of union therefore need to be properly considered.

The issues raised by EMU have been subject to much debate in Britain; and there is no lack of expert studies in academic and banking publications.[8] Part 2 of this paper sets out the proposals and discusses whether they are likely to be implemented. The paper is written from a British perspective and it should be noted that expert opinion in Britain, not only in Government but among banking and academic experts, has been more cautious about monetary union than in many Continental countries. There has perhaps been a greater awareness of the dangers if EMU goes wrong and a tendency to attach more value to the efficacy of exchange rate adjustment as a weapon in the economic armoury; whereas expert opinion in other countries is more concerned than in Britain at the potential instability of the Single Market in the absence of monetary integration. The issues are undoubtedly complex and require careful consideration: only an uncritical integrationist or an outright economic nationalist would regard the choice as easy. It is unfortunate, therefore, though perhaps inevitable on such a matter, that much of the discussion in the popular media has been emotive and partial in character. It has been dominated by the Eurosceptics and has been coloured by the fiasco of Britain's 1992 exit from the ERM, so that the full implications are not widely understood. Part 3 of this paper therefore attempts to set out a balanced view of these arguments.

Part 4 of the paper examines the regional implications of EMU. It is plain that no economic and monetary union can hope to succeed

---

[8]   See especially Gros, D, and N Thygesen (1992), *European Monetary Integration*, London: Longman; Kenen, P (1995), *Economic and Monetary Union in Europe*, Cambridge University Press; De Grauwe, P, and L Papdemos (1990), *The European Monetary System in the 1990s*, Harlow: Longman for Centre for European Policy Studies; CEC (1990), *One Market, One Money*, European Economy, No 44 Oct, Brussels; Lord Kingsdown (1995), *The Kingsdown Enquiry: Report by the ACE Working Group on the Implications of Monetary Union for Britain*, London: Action Centre for Europe.

in the long run unless all of the constituent countries, and indeed the principal regions, feel they derive benefit from it. If some parts were to gain, while others languish in economic difficulty, that would create serious political tensions, as the history of many of our present nation states illustrates clearly. If to differences of language, culture and history are added economic grievances, the dangers of fragmentation are particularly great, and prospects for success in such a union must indeed be poor. This has been recognised in Europe both in the Treaties and in the priority given to 'cohesion' policies.[9] EMU will carry integration to a more advanced stage and it is therefore often asserted that this implies a need for these policies to be further strengthened; indeed the report of the Delors Committee, which put forward the proposals for EMU, itself endorses this view.[10] This is a matter of importance to all Member States and is of particular interest to Scotland, which has been a beneficiary both of national and European regional policies.

[9] *Treaty on European Union* (TEU), especially Title XIV, Articles 130a to e.
[10] CEC (1989), *Report on Economic and Monetary Union in the European Community*, Luxembourg. The Committee comprised, in addition to the President of the Commission and some independent experts, the governors and chairmen of the national central banks.

II The Proposals For European Monetary Union

The Maastricht Plan

The scheme for EMU agreed at Maastricht and outlined in the Delors Report is well known and need only be briefly summarised.[11] Three stages are envisaged with the ultimate replacement of all national currencies with a single European currency. In stage 1 it was intended that all EU countries would join the ERM and reduce the fluctuation band of their currencies within the currency grid against the ECU to a maximum of 2.25%. Countries were to try to avoid further adjustment of exchange rates, although a final mutually agreed adjustment before parities were locked in stage 3 was provided for. In stage 2 the European Monetary Institute (EMI) was to be set up as the precursor of the European Central Bank; and there was to be increasingly close co-ordination of national monetary and economic policies. In stage 3 the parities for the currencies of participating states were to be locked irrevocably and, as soon as practical thereafter, to be replaced by a single currency. The earliest date at which stage 3 could be reached was to have been 1997, if a majority of countries was ready, but by 1999 EMU was to go ahead in any event with those countries that satisfied the convergence criteria, even if they were not a majority.

Events have of course turned out rather differently. The ERM crises of 1992 and 1993 resulted in the exit of the pound and the lira from the system (Greece never joined) and the devaluation of the peseta, the escudo and the Irish punt. 1993 saw the widening of the fluctuation margins to 15 percent, with the exception of the Netherlands which has continued to retain its currency within a fluctuation band of 2.25% against the D-mark. Despite this, the EMI was set up as planned and the EMU programme is now in stage 2. The recent European Council at Madrid has confirmed 1999 as the starting date for stage 3, as

[11] Treaty on European Union, loc cit; and CEC, op cit.

planned, for those Member States that are able adequately to satisfy the criteria. A decision is to be taken in 1998 on the initial membership.

The Convergence Criteria

There are four convergence criteria set out in Article 109j of the Treaty. These have to be taken together with Article 104c on excessive deficits, the reference values attached to these deficits and the Protocols on the excessive deficit procedure and on the convergence criteria:

Price Stability: participating countries must have a price performance that is sustainable and inflation that for one year before the examination has not exceeded by more than 1.5% that of the three best performing countries.

Government Financial Position: participating countries must have avoided excessive government deficits as defined by two tests: planned or actual budgetary deficits of not more than 3% of GDP, unless the ratio has declined substantially and comes close to this reference value; and a ratio of accumulated government debt of not more than 60% of GDP, unless the ratio is sufficiently diminishing and approaching this reference value at a satisfactory pace.

Exchange Rates: observance of the normal fluctuation margins provided for in the ERM for at least two years, without unilateral devaluation of the currency's bilateral central rate against the currency of any other Member State.

Long Term Interest Rates: as a test of the durability of convergence, for one year prior to examination the average long-term interest rate must not exceed that of the three best performing countries by more than two%, as measured by the rates on long-term government bonds.

None of these convergence criteria relate to unemployment or economic growth, which seems to show that those who drew them up, influenced perhaps by the Bundesbank's method of operation, were concerned more with monetary performance than with that of the real economy. This stems from the view, to which we will come later, that there is no trade-off between inflation and unemployment. But arguably unemployment should have been included in some form, since the inflation criterion is scarcely a sufficient test, if it can only be met at the cost of economic stagnation and unacceptable levels of unemployment.

An inflation criterion is clearly essential, if participating states are to maintain their competitive position in relation to each other. But it is not actually necessary for inflation to be everywhere the same, since the retail price index is made up from a mixture of goods and services, some of which are traded internationally and others are not. It is possible for countries that are growing fast and in the process of catching up on their competitors with high rates of productivity improvement in the manufacturing sector to maintain price stability in tradable goods at the same time as prices rise for non-tradable services (where the scope for productivity gain is much lower). Japan, for example, during the period of its very rapid growth, remained extremely competitive, although overall its economy had a significant rate of price increase, faster than some other industrialised countries.

The budgetary and debt criteria are intended to ensure that the participating member is not likely to create problems for the rest of the Union. The intention to operate the single currency with a monetary policy that is strictly non-inflationary could be put at risk by high levels of debt. In the past high debt levels have often led to part of that debt being financed through monetary expansion, with the result that the ratio of debt to GDP was reduced through inflation and at the expense of debt holders, who found that the real value of their assets declined. Furthermore, high and rising levels of debt on the part of some Member States could imperil the management of monetary policy within the Union by depressing bond prices, as well as requiring the high debt states to increase their levels of taxation to meet interest charges, thereby possibly damaging their growth prospects and the competitive position of their economies.

The remaining two criteria reinforce the first two, but principally that on inflation. They are also intended to give some assurance of long term durability. The exchange rate criterion has, of course, been made fairly meaningless following the widening of the ERM bands to 15% in 1993. 'Normal fluctuation margins' can now be interpreted as 15%, and would have to be if many countries are to qualify; but it is not the test of the steady exchange rates that was originally intended. Exchange rates are most likely to have been held if inflation performance has not seriously differed from that of the best performing countries, but this cannot absolutely be relied on. The crises involving the French franc have shown that speculative pressure can build up even where inflation performance is among the best. Long term interest rates converging on the best performers are a clear indication that the market anticipates neither excessive inflation nor exchange rate change.

These criteria are fairly crude and a number of obvious criticisms can be made of them. The budgetary criterion, on the assumption that GDP grows by approximately 3% a year, is set to ensure that annual deficits do not lead to an increase in outstanding debt. Those countries with faster growth of their GDP could maintain a constant debt ratio with a larger deficit, whereas those with nil or very little growth might have a rising debt ratio even if they did manage to keep their budget deficits to 3%. And where the deficit represents public sector investment that will yield a return in higher output, rather than revenue costs, it should not add to the debt ratio at all. Article 104c does make some allowance for this in saying that where a state fails the test the Commission in preparing its report will take into account whether the deficit exceeds investment expenditure.

The debt rule is perhaps even more questionable. For example, it is notable that the two countries that one could with most confidence expect to make a success of monetary union with Germany both fail the criteria. The Netherlands fails to meet the 60% debt criterion, although for more than a decade it has successfully pegged its currency so closely to the D-mark that it has effectively been in monetary union. The same applies to Austria, where the schilling has been successfully pegged to the D-mark for even longer, although it only joined the European Union in 1995, and neither its budget deficit nor its debt ratio is at present within the required limits. Belgium and Luxembourg have been in full monetary union with a single currency for a very long time, yet Belgium fails to meet both the 3% and 60% tests, whilst Luxembourg passes them comfortably. Britain has had a debt ratio of about 50% or lower only since 1975; it was 250% in 1945 and well above 100% throughout the inter-war period (Diagram 1). Yet the period 1919 to 1939 was one of falling rather than rising prices; and the period of very high debt during the 1950s and early 1960s saw the country successfully maintain a pegged exchange rate under the quasi-monetary union of Bretton Woods.

If the whole national debt is taken up within the country where it is issued, it amounts to no more than transfer payments from taxpayers to those who receive interest – many of whom are the same people. But if it is very large, the cost of interest payments could pre-empt other important elements of public expenditure; and, if part of the debt is held outside the country of issue, as may increasingly be expected in an integrated Europe, it will involve transfers from one Member State to

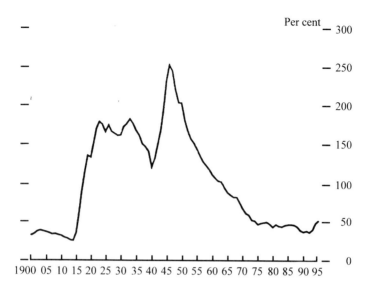

Diagram 1   Gross national debt as a percentage of GDP: 1900–95
Source: Bank of England

another. But more important than the absolute levels of each country's debt, which are largely an accident of history, is the need to prevent increases to levels that impose an unreasonable burden on future taxpayers in any Member State or imperil the Union's monetary stability. This it would certainly do if high debt led to monetisation, in an attempt to avoid high interest rates. How serious a problem a large debt is of course depends on the level of interest rates as well as the size of the debt. In this respect Belgium's debt, though higher than Italy's, is of less concern, because Belgian interest rates are well below those of Italy. With debt at 100% of GDP, a 10% interest rate means that each year the burden of servicing debt is 10% of GDP; with debt at 60% and interest rates of 6% the burden comes down to 3.6%. That Britain managed as well as it did in the post-war years when debt was so high, was largely due to the very low interest rates then prevailing and the fact that in real terms they were often negative. Thus, while it is a mistake to adopt too mechanistic a view on levels of debt that are acceptable for EMU, debt is a matter of legitimate concern. With the present high real interest rates, the general rise in debt levels in Europe in the early 1990s could be a potential problem and it therefore makes good sense to plan for their reduction, especially in countries where they are highest, particularly as many of these also have high interest rates.

More important, perhaps, than a country's ability to meet these criteria at the time of entry to EMU, is its behaviour once it is a member. At the start it is easy enough to say that a fiscally imprudent country does not qualify for entry; it is much more difficult to handle if it becomes fiscally imprudent after it is in. (This so-called 'free rider problem' is discussed more fully below.) The Treaty provides that there should be no bail-out for a country that allows its debt to rise imprudently, so that in the last analysis rising debt should carry a perception of increasing risk and a market penalty in higher interest rates. There is also provision for financial penalties in the form of non-interest bearing deposits or fines, which Theo Waigel, the German Finance Minister, has recently been advocating as a means of ensuring fiscal discipline. But these are very drastic steps: in either case the consequences would be very damaging to the cause of European union, and it is therefore hard to imagine these sanctions being used except in the most extreme circumstances.

If a Member State was ever allowed to default on its debt, the consequences to confidence, not only for it but for the rest of Europe, would be profoundly damaging. Equally a requirement to pay deposits, which would become fines in the absence of a quick return to the deficit criteria as interpreted by the Central Bank, could provoke massive resentment, even if ratified by the Council of Ministers. It would certainly play into the hands of those seeking to discredit the Union for their own political purposes. It is by deliberate design that the Central Bank is to be independent, and following the example of the Bundesbank, it is a requirement of EMU that national central banks should also be made independent. But it would test the acceptability of this to the limit to have a body that is not democratically accountable able to impose financial penalties on the elected governments of Member States.

It would also be perverse economically, unless the deficit was purely a consequence of irresponsible budgetary management. In most cases deficits are caused by the economic cycle or some unforeseen external shock and, as is shown later in this paper, flexibility in fiscal policy provides an essential automatic stabiliser. To impose an additional financial burden on a country at the very point when it is hit by recession and its deficit rises because of reduced tax revenue and higher social security expenditure, would be to make fiscal policy pro-cyclical instead of counter-cyclical. In its latest report the European Monetary Institute has suggested that the 3% budget deficit should be regarded as a maximum and that countries should generally aim for less than this.[12] This seems very rigid, and judging by what countries have achieved in the past, not least in the recession of the early 1990s, it seems unrealistic to expect it to be attained. A more flexible interpretation of the criteria is therefore needed. An average of 3% over the cycle might be more realistic and still quite tight; but this would be difficult to operate in practice, because countries could always plead that they were having a bad year and that next year or the year after would compensate.

Will EMU Happen?

Despite signs that the population in several Member States has become increasingly doubtful about EMU, the momentum in its favour remains strong among the political leadership of most countries. This applies even to Italy and Spain, which are still well away from meeting the convergence criteria.[13] The motivation is both political and economic. The former is the same as brought about the European Economic Community in the first place: the need to guarantee an end to strife; to enable the European countries to live comfortably within an ordered framework that prevents any one country from dominating the others; and to ensure that all can play their part in collective decisions. The term 'political union' clearly has different shades of meaning from one country to another: in Germany, for example, it is widely welcomed and probably means not much more than developing the framework just described; in France it is seen as a means of avoiding German domination of Europe; in Britain the expression frightens the horses – it has all sorts of implications about loss of national sovereignty, which is still more jealously guarded than it is elsewhere.

The economic motivation stems from a much clearer realisation in the other countries than in Britain that the Single Market is unstable without a single currency. Whereas many people in Britain saw the fiasco of sterling's exit from the ERM in 1992 as sealing the doom of the single currency project, in other countries the ERM crises were often

[12] See EMI (1995), *Progress towards Convergence*, Frankfurt; and European Commission (1995), *Report on Convergence in the European Union in 1995*, Brussels: Directorate General for Economic Affairs.

[13] See the *Financial Times* interview with the Spanish Prime Minister, Felipe Gonzàles, 6 Dec 1995, and the reaction of the Italian Government to remarks by the German Finance Minister before the 1995 Madrid Summit.

seen as making it more than ever necessary. If the Single Market (especially free capital movements) had destabilised the ERM, and if a return to controls on capital movements was unacceptable except as a temporary measure, the single currency was the logical goal. And generally other countries seem less concerned about the problems of living within the constraints of a single currency than either politicians or academic commentators in Britain.

The European Council agreement confirming that EMU would start in 1999 assumes that by July 1998, as required in Article 109j of the Treaty, the Commission and the EMI are able to report that a sufficient number qualify to make EMU appear worthwhile. In 1994 only Germany and Luxembourg unequivocally met all of the convergence criteria, and in 1995 there was only Luxembourg, Germany's budget deficit having risen to 3.5% of GDP in that year. However, as already explained, there is some flexibility permitted in the application of the fiscal criteria, and Ireland has been accepted as qualifying because it met the other criteria and its debt ratio, though exceeding 60%, was rapidly falling.

Ten countries – all except Italy, Spain, Portugal, Greece and the United Kingdom – met the inflation criterion in 1995, and the same ten are forecast to meet it in 1996 (Diagram 2 and appendix A). In the United Kingdom's case the inflation rate, though historically low, was 0.4% above the reference value in both years. Most countries that exceeded the reference value in 1995 have come closer to it in 1996, though inflation in Greece still exceeds it by 5.8%, and in Spain and Italy by 1.2% and 2.1% respectively; Portugal's inflation in 1996 is expected to be the same as the United Kingdom's – 3% compared with a reference value of 2.6. The long term interest rate criterion was met by ten countries in 1995 and eleven in 1996 (on the basis of the year October 1995 to September 1996). In both years the United Kingdom comfortably met the criterion (the exceptions were Sweden, Italy, Spain, Portugal and Greece in 1995, and the same countries without Sweden in 1996).

The principal problem, however, is with the deficit criterion (see Diagram 2 and Appendix A). In 1995 only Germany, France, Luxembourg, Finland and the United Kingdom had accumulated debt of less than 60% of GDP; and the forecasts for 1996 show an increase in both Germany and Finland so that it slightly exceeds 60%. Six countries have debt between 70% and 80%, but three have accumulated debt well in excess of 100% of GDP – Belgium (131), Italy (123), and

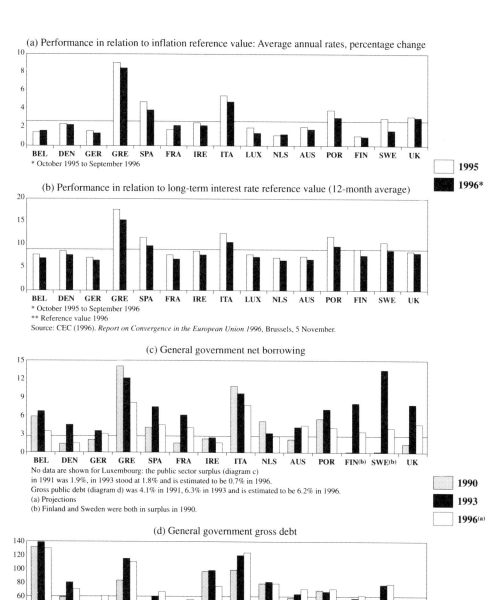

(a) Performance in relation to inflation reference value: Average annual rates, percentage change

* October 1995 to September 1996

1995
1996*

(b) Performance in relation to long-term interest rate reference value (12-month average)

* October 1995 to September 1996
** Reference value 1996
Source: CEC (1996). *Report on Convergence in the European Union 1996*, Brussels, 5 November.

(c) General government net borrowing

No data are shown for Luxembourg: the public sector surplus (diagram c)
in 1991 was 1.9%, in 1993 stood at 1.8% and is estimated to be 0.7% in 1996.
Gross public debt (diagram d) was 4.1% in 1991, 6.3% in 1993 and is estimated to be 6.2% in 1996.
(a) Projections
(b) Finland and Sweden were both in surplus in 1990.

1990
1993
1996(a)

(d) General government gross debt

Source: European Monetary Institute: Progress towards Convergence 1996.

Diagram 2 (a–d)

Greece (111). The 3% budget deficit test was met only by Denmark, Ireland and Luxembourg in 1995; and in 1996 the forecast shows these three joined by the Netherlands. Belgium, Germany, France, Portugal, Finland and Sweden are forecast to have deficits at or below 4% (i.e. within 1% of the reference value) in 1996; the remainder range from Austria (4.3%) to Greece (7.9%), with the United Kingdom at 4.6%. The average budget deficit in Member States was forecast to be closer to the reference value in 1996 than in 1995, and it therefore is possible that most, if not all, of the ten countries with deficits of of 4% or less could meet it by 1998. But it is one of the unsatisfactory features of these criteria that any assumptions about the remaining countries coming closer to satisfying them depend upon the continued expansion of their economies out of recession. If there were another downturn, these deficits would rise again; and attempts to force them down to 3% in such circumstances would only turn recession into slump, thereby making the deficits worse.

How many participants would make EMU worthwhile? Although, under the Treaty, stage 3 starts in any event in 1999 with whatever countries qualify, it is hard to see the Council adhering to this if only about three countries qualify and if there is opposition from several large Member States. The key is France. Without France, a union which might be limited to Germany, the Benelux states and Austria would be little more than a D-mark zone with a new currency. France's problem is its budget deficit, which would have met the test at the time of Maastricht but has risen considerably in the 1990s as a result of recession and overspending on various social security funds. Attempts are being made to address this, though at the cost of widespread industrial disruption, and some sleight of hand over accounting conventions, and the French Government claims that it can meet the budgetary criteria in time for a 1999 start. On that basis, assuming that the budgetary position in the Netherlands, Austria and Finland improves and enables the level of debt in those countries to be judged acceptable, and assuming further that an understanding view can be taken of Belgium, which although meeting the criteria on inflation, interest rates and currency stability has a very high debt, a monetary union of seven might start with Germany, France, Netherlands, Finland, Belgium, Luxembourg and Austria.

To these seven could be added the United Kingdom, Denmark, and Ireland, since all of these could be expected adequately to meet the criteria by 1999. But the growth of Euroscepticism is now so strong in

Britain that the chances of the United Kingdom joining must be judged remote. With such an articulate opposition, both in Parliament and the press, even a different Government with stronger pro-European leadership would have difficulty in embarking on a project that involves a major short term upheaval combined with considerable risk and with benefits that would only be apparent in the long term. If the United Kingdom stays out, the chances must be that Denmark will do the same. Denmark obtained an 'opt-out' from the monetary union clauses of the Maastricht Treaty at the Edinburgh meeting of the European Council in 1992, following the negative vote in the first Danish referendum on the Treaty. But the terms are different from Britain's opt-out: whereas the British Government has retained the right to either join or stay out of EMU, subject to the approval of Parliament, Denmark's opt-out is on the basis that it will stay out. If the Government decides that after all it would be in the country's interest to join, this would be subject not only to approval in the Danish Parliament but to a further popular referendum. Recently this situation has been causing concern both to the Government coalition and to the leading opposition parties who believe that Denmark's economy may suffer from staying out. According to Mogens Lykketoft, the Finance Minister, the economy is extremely stable, is being run on policies closely parallel to Germany and is likely to meet the Maastricht criteria in time for entry in 1999.[14] All that opting out may therefore achieve is a higher rate of interest for the Danish krone than for the European single currency. But the chances of securing a favourable referendum result to enable Denmark to opt-in depend on a campaign to convince the electorate of the advantages, and this would be easier if Britain joined as well.

Ireland, on the other hand, did not negotiate an opt out. It meets the criteria, apart from the debt ratio; and although this is well over 60% of GDP, it is declining fast. In September 1994, under the terms of the Treaty, the Commission submitted its report, as required, on the countries that failed to qualify under the criteria; it submitted reports on ten of the then twelve Member States, the exceptions being Luxembourg and Ireland. This remains the position, and it means that in each of the last two years Ireland has been accepted as qualifying. Assuming this situation is maintained, it could therefore be required to join in accordance with the Treaty. This could create a problem for Ireland, if its economy were tied irrevocably to a strong European currency, while Britain, its main trading partner, stayed outside and

---

[14] As reported in the *Financial Times*, 27 Nov 1995.

sterling continued to depreciate. Therefore, although entry should not be ruled out – Ireland did after all join the ERM when Britain did not – the potential difficulties of this situation might lead to an Irish decision to stay out. In practice it is hard to imagine that the other members would insist on a strict interpretation of the Treaty, if entry would be damaging to Ireland and if a decision to stay out was supported by the Irish Parliament.

If this analysis is accepted, France is the key to monetary union happening in a meaningful fashion at all; but the United Kingdom, apart from determining her own fate, may be the key to whether it is a union of seven or ten. Whatever happens Sweden, Italy, Spain, Portugal and Greece are unlikely to be ready to join monetary union in 1999.[15] Sweden, Spain and Portugal might have hopes of doing so relatively soon thereafter; Italy's problems are partly political and more intractable, while Greece seems a very long way from adequately satisfying the criteria.

[15] Since this was written Italy and Spain in particular have been pressing hard to join EMU in the first wave, and have taken measures to correct their budget deficits. But it remains the author's view, mainly on grounds of inflation, that they should not join in 1999.

III   The Case For And Against Monetary Union

The Arguments in Favour

Many people in Britain see EMU as an unnecessary additional piece of integration without appreciating how it follows from earlier steps in the process of European economic integration. They simply do not understand why such an ambitious project has been embarked upon. Attitudes, particularly the conviction that it will give rise to serious, but usually undefined, problems, have been influenced by the Government's manoeuvrings and expression of its own doubts on the proposals. These include the 1989 rival scheme put forward by the Treasury for a 'hard ECU', the negotiation of Britain's opt-out from the terms of the Maastricht Treaty, Britain's departure from the ERM, subsequent Ministerial criticisms of the shortcomings of that scheme and attempts to delay the starting date of EMU.[16] The following paragraphs therefore set out the arguments for monetary union.

(a) Greater Ease and Reduced Cost of Transactions

Most people recognise that EMU would bring a gain both in the ease and cost of inter-country transactions. This gain could be substantial: studies by the Commission estimated it at 0.5% of Europe's GDP.[17] Just as a money economy is a great step forward from one based on barter, and much more efficient, so a single currency in a single market is much more efficient than a plurality. The risks, uncertainties and inhibitions that previously applied to trade across national frontiers are removed and for the first time such business becomes no more difficult or risky than that conducted within a single Member State. It is true

---

[16]   HM Treasury (1989), *An Evolutionary Approach to Economic and Monetary Union*, London.

[17]   CEC (1990), op cit, p 21.

that many of these risks and uncertainties can be insured against, but at a cost that becomes unnecessary with a single currency. The resources can then be deployed to other more directly beneficial uses and trade can be facilitated, thereby increasing the gains from specialisation and from scale of operation.

(b) The Single Market Requires Monetary Stability

The most important consideration, however, is that a single market requires monetary stability if it is to become properly integrated, or possibly even if it is to survive.[18] Flexible and constantly changing exchange rates would be compatible with a single market if they always truly reflected the economic fundamentals of Member States' economies. The situation might be confusing, but no producer should feel that competition was unfair. In the real world, however, exchange rates for currencies can and do depart a long way, and for lengthy periods, from levels based on the underlying strength of the economies to which they relate. They are subject to Government policy (deliberate or otherwise) and are greatly influenced by speculators. Currencies in which the market has confidence get driven up and often overshoot economically realistic values; weak currencies are in contrast driven down. And every time there is an international currency crisis speculators tend to move from the weak to the strong. Thus, at the present pound/D-mark exchange rate, unit labour costs in German manufacturing industry are nearly twice as high as in Britain, yet German productivity is estimated to be only about 20% higher than British.[19]

As a result of seemingly wanton currency movements, the competitive position between firms in different countries is altered: producers feel that the terms on which they compete for business are no longer fair; and those considering investment in Europe find that the advantages of locations in different states vary unpredictably. If, therefore, Governments dismantle not only their customs barriers but non-tariff barriers as well, in accordance with the Single European Act,

[18] Padoa-Schioppa, T, (1987), *Efficiency, Stability and Equity*, Oxford University Press, p 76; Goodhart, C A E, (1989), *The Delors Report*, LSE typescript; CEC (1990), op cit, p 17.

[19] *Competitiveness: Forging Ahead*, Cm 2867, London: HMSO (1995), pp 11, 33, 104; and Oulton, N, (1994), *Labour Productivity and Unit Labour Costs in Manufacturing: the UK and its Competitors*, National Institute Economic Review, no 148 (May).

they can expect widespread complaints from businesses in countries adversely affected whenever exchange rates move without apparent economic justification.

The complaints by French industrialists since 1992 about unfair competition from Italy, Spain and the United Kingdom illustrate this point. Despite the widening of ERM bands to 15% in 1993, France has maintained the franc fort, the close relationship with the D-mark. With lower inflation than Germany and a stronger balance of payments, successive French Governments believed that the economic situation did not justify devaluation. Furthermore, having been a country with a poor inflation record in the 1970s and early 1980s, and having got that inflation firmly under control, they did not want to risk losing ground that had been won at considerable cost. But if the D-mark is now overvalued the attempt by the French to maintain the D-mark parity of the franc has resulted in it being overvalued too against sterling and the lira, which have substantially depreciated since leaving the ERM in 1992, and the peseta, which, though still in the ERM, has been devalued several times. If that is so, the latter countries are exporting their unemployment to France and Germany.

It is never easy in these circumstances to establish the validity of such arguments. But so long as exchange rates can be pushed around so easily, both Governments and businesses will believe competition is unfair. The result is likely to be either that they fail properly to implement the Single European Act or that, in time, they create more rather than less artificial barriers to trade. In the long-run, therefore, a stable and ordered system of exchange rates, if not a single currency, is essential for the effective operation of the Single Market.

The onus is therefore on those who would reject monetary union to show by what other means this problem can be tackled. When the Treaty of Rome was signed, the Bretton Woods system was still in operation and the problem of disorderly exchange rates was not an issue. It became one in 1971 when that system collapsed. The creation of the European Monetary System, and in particular the ERM, which became operational in 1979, established sufficient stability for the European Community to develop throughout the 1980s, providing the momentum for the Single European Act. But the Single European Act itself carried the seeds of the destruction of that system: as early as 1987 the report of the Padoa-Schioppa Committee for the European Commission pointed out that the ERM was unlikely to survive the liberalisation of capital movements, and similar predictions were made by British experts.[20] Padoa-Schioppa termed the resulting situation an attempt at coexistence by the 'inconsistent quartet': free trade; full capital mobility; fixed or managed exchange rates; and national autonomy in monetary policy. Capital mobility without restriction makes currency speculation easier; fixed or managed exchange rates could make such speculation a one way bet for the speculator; and differences in national monetary policies could provide the trigger. The only solutions to this inherently unstable situation are: the restoration of exchange controls or other impediments to capital mobility, which would conflict with the objectives of the Single Market; the adoption of floating rates or wider bands, which has in the event occurred but in Padoa-Schioppa's view carry a threat to the Single Market; or the adoption of an integrated European monetary policy.

The events of 1992 and 1993 simply confirmed this diagnosis. It is perhaps surprising that the British Government, in strongly supporting the Single Market including the lifting of exchange controls, apparently did not foresee these difficulties. The crisis arose sooner than might otherwise have happened, because of the additional strains imposed by German reunification and the international recession. But the conclusion is clear: with the rapid and substantial monetary movements that can now take place in and out of currencies, a narrow band ERM-type system cannot continue with freedom of capital mobility and independent monetary policies. Although currency speculation has always been a problem and controls on capital movements could never be more than partially effective, recent research has shown that the dismantling of such controls has both reduced the ability of Governments to counter pressure and the time available in which to mount a defence.[21]

(c) Economic Growth, Inflation and Unemployment

There are several reasons for expecting a single currency to improve the overall performance of the economy. First, the greater ease of transactions, already referred to, would enable the benefits of integration to be carried much further than would be likely otherwise. The Cecchini Report on the effects of the Single European Act showed the potential

[20] Padoa-Schioppa, T, (1989), op cit, p 76; Goodhart, C A E, (1989), op cit, p 8; CEC (1990), op cit, p 9.
[21] Eichengreen, B, A Rose and C Wyploz (1994), *Speculative Attacks on Pegged Exchange Rates*, CEPR Discussion Paper No 1060.

gain to be of the order of 7% of the European GDP.[22] While one is entitled to some scepticism over precise estimates of this kind, the conclusion that gains could be substantial was accepted by all member countries. A significant proportion of these arose in the financial sector, and although many of the non-tariff barriers in this sector will be reduced as a result of the Single European Act, the gains cannot be fully achieved, particularly so far as individuals are concerned, without a single currency. In other sectors too, because of the reduction of risk and uncertainty, bolder and more rational investment decisions will be taken with benefits for economic growth.

There is also a potential gain from reduction in interest costs. Monetary union can be expected to reduce nominal interest costs if, as proposed, monetary policy is non-inflationary and is based on that of Germany, particularly if the Bundesbank's inflation record can be maintained by the new Central Bank. But monetary union also provides an opportunity to reduce real interest rates, since these are partly a reflection of exchange risk. Real interest rates are at present high by historical standards, perhaps partly because of currency volatility, and lower rates could do much to stimulate investment and improve growth prospects.

But there is a third way in which the present disorderly pattern of exchange rates between the major currencies impedes economic growth. European prosperity and low unemployment require a European currency that can be managed in relation to other world currencies so as to ensure that the European economy is competitive. A single currency would serve a much larger population than the D-mark, even if it only applied to a core group of six or seven countries, and being more broadly based, it would be less easily pushed up by speculative pressure. It would be managed on behalf of Europe as a whole and the Euro would soon be seen, along with the dollar and the yen, as one of the three major international currencies. This might in turn lead to the present Group of Seven major economic powers becoming a Group of Three for purposes of international currency management and the G7 being retained or expanded to provide a second tier less involved in major decisions. By thus strengthening Europe's hand in international discussions, the single currency would enable it to play a more effective part in maintaining an orderly and competitive pattern of exchange rates.

Many of those who argued in the past for the adoption of a flexible

[22]   Cecchini, P, M Catimat and A Jacquemin (1988), *The European Challenge 1992: The Benefits of the Single Market*, Aldershot: Gower.

exchange rate system believed that the need to maintain fixed rates had a stultifying effect on growth and unemployment, and that it could also result in the transmission of inflation from one state to another. In the event the reverse has been the case: flexible rates have been accompanied by slower growth, more unemployment and more inflation than occurred under the Bretton Woods system, or prior to 1914 under the Gold Standard. This is not a coincidence. Experience of devaluations has shown that in many cases the effects reach through in a comparatively short period into higher inflation, quickly wiping out any competitive gain. Indeed if a cycle of inflation begins, deflationary measures of increasing intensity have to be imposed, which reduce growth and raise unemployment. A system that brings internal currency stability to Europe and enables the exchange rate between a single European currency and the other major world currencies to more accurately reflect economic fundamentals could therefore be a major element in a strategy to improve European growth and reduce unemployment.

The Arguments Against

The case against monetary union is based on two distinct sets of arguments. The first relates to differences in economic performance and asserts that it will not work without imposing damaging strains on some of the participants. The second claims that monetary union necessarily requires nation states to hand over powers to an extent that results in an unacceptable loss of sovereignty.

(a) Differing Economic Performance

Economies may find it difficult, for a number of reasons, to prosper together in an economic and monetary union, where they are subject to the same monetary policy and cannot look to exchange rate adjustment to take the strain of differences in their circumstances. In the first place it is essential to enter at the right exchange rate when rates are fixed. This is not so easy as might be thought and Britain's experience with the ERM is salutary in this respect. But, even if one gets this right, problems may subsequently arise because of differing tendencies towards inflation, differing exposure and reaction to external shocks and differing potential for economic growth, stemming either from greater availability of labour resources in some countries or more rapid gains in productivity. All of these could give rise to economic imbalance between countries, creating in effect a 'regional' problem at the level of nation states. This aspect of the issue is discussed in Part 4 of this paper. Suffice to say at this stage that if such problems become severe, they would have the potential to create not only regional economic imbalance on a large scale, but could give rise to pressures which put the continued existence of EMU at risk.

Inflation has already been touched on since, alone of the above, it features among the Maastricht convergence criteria. If one country suffers higher rates of inflation than the others after EMU, it will quickly find its economy uncompetitive; the consequence of which will be stagnation and unemployment until prices can be brought back into line. Those who regard inflation as purely, or even predominantly, a monetary phenomenon may regard this as a fairly transitory problem, given that all Member States will have the same monetary policy. But there are institutional features, such as trade union structures and attitudes, and degree of acceptance of inflation on the part of employers and consumers, which affect a country's propensity for inflation and the balance between inflation and unemployment. Eventually these attitudes and expectations may become very similar within a monetary union, but that is likely to take time and the transition may be slow and uncomfortable. Success is therefore much more likely if genuine and sustainable convergence has been achieved in advance, not simply similar rates of inflation at the time of entry to EMU.

Differing reaction to shocks or exposure to them and differing growth potential require, within EMU, adequate scope to continue management of the economy at the level of the Member State. The economic cycle may not be identically phased in all countries (in the 1990s, for example the recession hit Britain earlier than France or Germany); countries may differ considerably in the structure of their economies and may therefore respond differently to external events; some countries may be more affected than others by an energy price rise or by the collapse of a major industry; or institutional differences, such as the prevalence in Britain of short-term personal borrowing or variable rate mortgages and in Germany of long-term fixed rate borrowing, may result in very different responses by the economy to the same policy measures.[23] For example a rise in short-term interest rates that may be right for conditions in

[23] McCrone, G, and M Stephens (1995), *Housing Policy in Britain and Europe*, London: UCL Press, pp 240–50.

Germany may have a much more drastic effect on consumers' expenditure in Britain.

Within an existing nation state some of these differences have been ironed out and for those that remain there are safety valves in freedom of capital movements and substantial inter-regional migration. The Single Market provides for both of these, but realistically it is unlikely that inter-country labour migration will be either acceptable or other than a very modest safety valve for a long time to come. Nor, for social and political reasons, is it desirable that it should be. The other corrective measures within a nation state are inter-regional fiscal transfers and regional policy. These are discussed in Part 4, but the EU lacks the former and the latter, though receiving increased resources, has enough to cope with in the existing regional disparities of the Union. It is therefore fair to conclude that without substantial continuing scope for macroeconomic management at the level of the nation state, much greater than for regions within a country, the strain on monetary union might be too great to enable it to survive.

(b) The 'Free Rider' Problem

With separate currencies, Governments of Member States are restrained from irresponsible fiscal policies by the effect these policies would have on their balance of payments and exchange rates. If they are irresponsible in running consistently high budget deficits, their volume of outstanding debt increases, implying high tax burdens to meet future interest charges, and unrestrained public spending is likely to boost demand thereby causing the balance of payments to go into deficit. Both problems will undermine confidence in the currency; but currency depreciation, although adding to domestic inflation in the country concerned, has only a limited effect on other countries under a system of floating rates.

With a common currency a Member State that behaved in this way would not face the same sanction. It would still have to tax future generations to meet interest charges on a high public debt, but with no separate currency its profligacy would not be checked by fear of depreciation. Instead, if it was large and sufficiently profligate, so that its debt came greatly to exceed its share of the Union's population, it would in the end risk undermining the successful management of the single currency. In federal countries there is not generally a central government control of borrowing by the component states or provinces other than the fear of ultimate insolvency, and some people have argued that it is not necessary in EMU either.[24] But this really depends on making the no-bail out rule effective, so that countries with high debt are disciplined by the market through high interest rates. As explained above, for the reasons already discussed, it is not easy to see how this could be adhered to in practice, nor how the various sanctions proposed could be applied. This therefore remains a worrying aspect of managing EMU. In normal circumstances one can probably rely on Governments to behave responsibly; but circumstances are not always normal. The problem highlights the difficulty of having a monetary union without a political and fiscal union.

(c) Economic Sovereignty

One of the arguments most frequently heard in Britain is that, since EMU involves transfer of control over monetary and exchange rate policy to the European Central Bank, it represents a major loss of national economic sovereignty. Furthermore transfer of these major levers of economic management means not only that they shift from the national to the European level but that they are acquired by a body that is not democratically accountable even to the European Parliament. If the policies of the ECB were thought to be unacceptable or misguided, because, for example, they led to intolerable levels of unemployment, the only sanction open to national governments would be to replace individual directors at the end of their appointed term.

But this is not quite such an extreme step as it may appear. Of course the adoption of a single currency takes the process of integration further than with previous systems, and makes it difficult and costly to opt out again if the policies being followed are not to one's taste. But some transfer of economic sovereignty is involved in any system of fixed exchange rates, such as Bretton Woods and ERM. A major difference with EMU, and one that should be an advantage to participating countries, is that the responsibility for monetary policy will rest with an all European central bank, which is required to have regard to economic conditions throughout Member States, rather than the central bank of one country – the Bundesbank in the case of ERM and the Federal Reserve under Bretton Woods. It was precisely because the Bundesbank, under its statutes, had to determine its policies in the light of

---

[24] See for example Davies, G, (1989), *Britain and the European Monetary Question*, Economic Study No 1, London: IPPR.

German conditions alone, and not those of other ERM countries, that the system came under such immense strain in 1992 and 1993 following German reunification. Moreover, it is an increasingly held view that monetary policy should be distanced from the political cycle, as a means of ensuring that inflation is controlled. It is for this reason that countries are required under the Maastricht Treaty to make their central banks independent; and quite separately the arguments for this have also been put forward in Britain with support from more than one former Chancellor of the Exchequer.

EMU does not require loss of national control in fiscal policy, except in so far as the limits on the budget deficit under the convergence criteria reduce scope for independent action. The Single Market, however, already places significant constraints on fiscal policy. It was intended that excise duties and VAT would be harmonised within agreed bands: these are much wider and less restrictive than originally envisaged, with the result that substantial variations in both VAT rates and duties remain. But the abolition of tax frontiers between Member States means that there is now pressure to remove major differences in these taxes, since their existence leads to distortions in shopping patterns across national frontiers. As an island, Britain can maintain such differences more easily than many of the other countries, although the trade in alcohol and other commodities across the Channel from Calais shows that there are limits even in Britain's case. There is no requirement to harmonise direct taxation, but even it cannot be set in complete disregard of tax levels in other countries, since both capital and highly skilled labour are mobile between Member States. For this reason few would now consider it practicable for Britain to maintain a marginal rate of income tax of 98%, as it was for some years in the 1970s, or for Sweden to revert to the very high marginal levels of taxation that applied in the 1980s.

But while these are very real limitations on national governments' fiscal policy, most of them have existed for some years. And there is still considerable scope for independent action, as is shown by the massive increases in tax revenue resulting from the British budgets of 1993 and 1994, amounting to a total of £15 billion, which were achieved without any change in actual rates of personal income taxation. The recent increase in the French VAT rate illustrates the same point.

The effects of loss of economic sovereignty should therefore not be exaggerated. Economic policy has always been constrained by the need to take account of circumstances in other countries with which Britain trades. And the whole process of economic integration since the original foundation of the EEC has reduced freedom of action by nation states in economic policy; it has done so because Member States recognised that the benefits of integration outweighed this loss, and that in any event such freedom in a relatively small independent state is often more apparent than real. Monetary union is no different: what is lost to the nation state with EMU is chiefly the freedom to go on making its currency increasingly worthless as a means of making up for other deficiencies in economic management. And the quasi-unions of the past – the Gold Standard and Bretton Woods – also involved Governments tying their hands. Economic sovereignty is not an absolute which, like virginity, one either has or has lost. The issue is simply whether the undoubted loss in freedom of action that is involved in transferring responsibility for monetary and exchange rate policy to the European level is more than offset by the economic benefits that a common currency could make possible.

(d) Macroeconomic Policy

Nevertheless it is an inevitable consequence of transferring responsibility for monetary and exchange rate policy to the European level that nation states will have to rely rather more on fiscal policy to balance their economies. To some extent monetary and fiscal policy are alternative ways of achieving balance in the economy; and if the former is no longer available, greater reliance will have to be placed on the latter. It is not clear, particularly in the light of the EMI's rigid interpretation of the 3% deficit criterion, that enough scope would remain to nation states to conduct an effective macroeconomic policy by this means. That might not matter so much if a proper macroeconomic policy also comes to be conducted at the European level so that responsibility for such policy is genuinely shared between European institutions and national governments. The important issue is not therefore loss of sovereignty by the nation state but the need to ensure that, if functions are handed over, an effective policy can be conducted.

As the European economies have become more integrated, independent macroeconomic policies have become increasingly difficult to operate, because of spill-over effects from one country to another. The more open an economy, the less power a national government has to manage demand without precipitating a balance of payments crisis or exporting its inflation and unemployment problems to other countries.

The French experience in the early 1980s, when attempts made to stimulate the economy unilaterally had to be abandoned, illustrated this clearly.

Macroeconomic policy could, however, be much more effective at the European level. For most EU Member States, the largest share of their trade is with each other, so that the spill-over to third countries would be much smaller for the EU as a whole, more akin to the situation in the United States. As the Padoa-Schioppa Report has said:

> If all Europe expanded at once...the current account consequences would be less than half as large as for a typical country, the multiplier effects would be larger and hence the budget impact less unfavourable.[25]

So far this aspect of EMU has received much less attention than it deserves and known positions are not encouraging. The intention seems to be to run monetary policy along the lines followed in Germany by the Bundesbank, with priority given to the avoidance of inflation without mention of employment; fiscal policy would be constrained by the 3% deficit rule; and little has been said about the need, referred to earlier, to manage the exchange rate against other major currencies so as to ensure that the European economy is competitive. While it may be true in the long run that there is no trade off between inflation and unemployment – though this view is by no means universally accepted – it is certainly not true of the short run, and the short run can last for many years. There is a danger that if the Central Bank is required to give priority to the control of inflation without regard for other considerations, it may achieve its objective by running an excessively tight monetary policy with high interest rates that impede growth and result in an overvalued currency. Unless these matters are given proper attention, not only will a major opportunity for producing a more effective policy be lost, but the results could be very damaging.

It is because of these difficulties that some people, both those in favour of EMU and those opposed, have argued that monetary union is not practicable without some degree of political union. Much closer cooperation on all aspects of economic policy and management will certainly be required if it is to succeed. In democratic countries, the population will not accept for long policies decided by a nominated body that they cannot hold accountable, if they feel they are suffering from those policies or if they believe them to be mistaken. This makes it all the more necessary that the Council of Ministers itself should

[25]   Op cit, p 135.

THE CASE FOR AND AGAINST MONETARY UNION 33

recognise the need for a European dimension to macroeconomic policy, of which the policies of ECB would form a part. Although there are major potential benefits from EMU, they are long term, whereas the adjustments required for a single currency could be quite painful for some countries and will be felt immediately. If the project is to succeed, and not result in a major set-back, it is therefore essential that these issues are addressed and that people see clearly how EMU is to enhance European prosperity rather than turn into a monetary and fiscal straitjacket.

The Consequences of a Partial Monetary Union

If the analysis earlier in this paper is accepted, an EMU starting in 1999 is unlikely to involve more than a core group of about seven countries. EMU would therefore split the countries of the European Union into two divisions. Indeed, since there is unlikely to be a moment when all 15 countries are simultaneously ready for entry, this is likely to be the position even if a much later date is chosen. It can be argued that such a split does no more than recognise the political realities of Europe. In the enlarged Union some countries are more integrationist and some economies are more advanced than others; it is no longer the relatively homogeneous Community of six countries that signed the Treaty of Rome in 1957. If the Union is to continue to make progress, perhaps those countries that feel ready to advance should be allowed to do so without waiting for the slower members of the convoy.

As compared with having no EMU, there could be advantages in such an arrangement. In the first place it would get it started. Secondly, the European Central Bank, unlike the Bundesbank in the ERM, would be required by statute to have regard to conditions in all of the participating states, if not the whole European Union, in setting its monetary policy. Thirdly, the new European currency, even if only for six or seven countries, would still have a larger role both in Europe and in the rest of the world than the D-mark, and the ECB could play a substantial role in the management of international monetary conditions. But it would be a mistake for those countries that do not join to think that their position would be unchanged. Inevitably they would be even more affected by the policies pursued by the ECB than they are at present by the Bundesbank.

But there would also be disadvantages with such a system. First, a divided Europe would do little to solve the problem of stability between currencies in the Single Market. Although monetary stability would be achieved among the core members, they could still face what they would regard as unfair competition from those in the outer rim, whom they might accuse of engaging in beggar-my-neighbour devaluations. Exchange rates between these national currencies and the single currency are likely to remain volatile unless a new ERM type system is established to stabilise them. Little thought has so far been given to how this problem should be handled. A system of narrow band pegged or managed exchange rates is no more likely to be successful against speculative pressure than the ERM was in 1992, unless some limitations on freedom of capital movements are reintroduced. Many would regard this as a retrograde step, and it may be more practical to continue ERM mark 2, with the wide 15% bands, but with each country aiming for currency stability within much narrower limits though prepared to yield temporarily to pressure when it occurs.

A two-tier system of this kind is most likely to be acceptable if it is regarded as a transition stage, with the outer rim currencies joining EMU relatively soon after it is started. But thought needs to be given to whether special measures are necessary to ease the path of these currencies into EMU. As Paul de Grauwe has pointed out, the irony is that it would be much easier for countries to meet the convergence criteria inside EMU than outside.[26] The adoption of the new single currency would be the best way for countries to break the cycle of inflationary expectations attached to their existing national currencies; and lower interest rates, by cutting the cost of servicing debt, would make it easier to meet the budget deficit criterion and bring down the volume of accumulated debt. Indeed the danger is rather that exclusion from EMU would further weaken confidence in the inflationary credentials of national currencies; it would give a signal that these countries wished to continue to rely on devaluations, with the result that their interest rates would rise. This EMU trap could make it more difficult than ever for the outer rim countries to meet the criteria for joining.

If Britain decides not to join, not because it fails the criteria but because it does not want to, it is perhaps less likely to be caught in this trap. But apart from being an expression of national independence, the markets will still assume that Britain does not want to join because it

[26]   De Grauwe, P, (1995), Unpublished paper delivered at the Europa Institute, Edinburgh, 1995, and also an article in the *Financial Times*, 17 Oct 1995.

wants to retain freedom to adjust its exchange rates; and it will be assumed that that means periodic devaluation. Provided that the single currency, like the D-mark, establishes a good non-inflationary record, Britain is therefore also likely to have to pay a premium in higher interest rates to compensate for currency risk. Unless it is intended never to join, it would therefore make sense, whether or not there is a formal ERM type link, to manage the economy so that the value of the pound is kept as steady in relation to the new single currency as possible. In that way confidence in sterling's ability to retain its value would gradually be built up, with benefits in lower interest rates, and Britain could be assured of a relatively easy transition to EMU when it did decide to join. But as the Danish Government presently seem to feel and as several members of the ERM have discovered, this policy has its drawbacks. In some respects it combines the worst of both worlds: it means forswearing policy freedom but interest rates still have to be kept above those of the anchor currency because it is regarded as the safer currency.

In addition to these considerations there are the possible effects of a two-tier system on the flow of inward investment. This is of special importance to Britain because in proportion to GDP the United Kingdom is much more heavily engaged than any of the other countries both as an overseas investor and as a host for direct inward investment. Over the years 1981 to 1991 the average outward flow at about 3% of GDP was larger than the inward flow, although the latter was close to 2% of GDP.[27] For the Scottish economy, with its heavy dependence on electronics and North Sea oil, inward investment is of even greater importance; indeed in 1992 36% of manufacturing output and 25% by employment were accounted for by foreign-owned firms.[28] It is essential for the health of the economy that this flow of inward investment should be maintained, and that is heavily dependent on Britain's position in relation to Europe, because the reason that so many of the inward investors are attracted to Britain is that they regard it as a good location from which to serve the European market. If this link is put in doubt, much of this flow would switch to other European countries, and British investment in other countries, already high, would increase.

British decisions on EMU could affect this because of the signals they

[27] *Competitiveness etc*, Cm 2867 (1995), p 26.
[28] Scottish Office (1995), *Statistical Bulletin: Industry Series*, GSS Paper, May, Table 6b.

might give to potential investors. What they want is to be assured that Britain will remain a full participating member of the Single Market and a competitive location from which to serve it. That could best be met if Britain joined EMU and really achieved convergence without having to impose a long period of deflationary measures resulting in high unemployment. The next best thing would be to maintain a competitive position outside EMU while retaining full access to the Single Market. But, particularly in the light of strong Eurosceptic pressure, the dangers are that Britain's decision not to join EMU would be seen as a sign that Britain was half-hearted about its European commitment and might eventually withdraw; or that core members of EMU might become increasingly reluctant to dismantle non-tariff barriers to permit real freedom of trade because they regarded a weak or devaluing pound as a source of unfair competition in the European market.

Rather similar considerations apply to the financial sector. Finance is a very important industry for Britain, and London is by far the biggest financial centre in Europe. Indeed until the late 1960s sterling was the most widely used currency for international purposes, apart from the dollar. London is therefore the natural financial capital of Europe, but its chances of being the chosen site for the ECB were remote after Britain served notice at Maastricht that it might not want to participate in the single currency. Of course London will deal in Euros, just as it does in Eurodollars, and there are examples of important financial centres – Switzerland, Hong Kong – that are not part of a large currency area. The issue is as much psychological as economic and the consequences are therefore difficult to forecast. But it would be surprising if Frankfurt does not gain considerably as a financial centre as a consequence of becoming the site for the ECB. Indeed it could be, if Britain chooses to remain outside the single currency system, that financial institutions see more and more advantage in siting themselves in Frankfurt rather than London. If that were to happen, the loss to the British economy over the longer term could be very serious.

IV   The Regional
Implications of EMU

One of the concerns most frequently heard about EMU is that it may either create or aggravate problems of regional economic imbalance. Were this to happen, it could have grave consequences not only for the success of EMU but for European economic integration generally. If political tensions leading to the disruption of the Union are to be avoided, it is essential for all countries and major regions to feel that they are better off within the Union than they would be outside. This does not require an equalisation of living standards; indeed that would be impossible to achieve except in the very long term, if ever. But it does mean that, as Europe grows in prosperity, the benefits need to be widely shared.

The importance of this issue is recognised in the emphasis given to it in the Maastricht Treaty.[29] Amongst other provisions the Treaty requires the Commission to submit a report every three years on the progress made towards achieving economic and social cohesion and the manner in which the various means provided for have contributed to it.

This issue is of particular concern to Scotland. The Scottish economy has experienced, over the last half century, a painful process of economic restructuring, as older industries have had to be replaced with new forms of economic activity. Scotland is therefore no stranger to problems of unemployment and net emigration and has benefited both from United Kingdom regional policy and from the structural funds of the European Union. In addition Scotland's location is unquestionably on the periphery of the European market. That is not as serious a handicap as is sometimes suggested – the success of inward investment in Scotland confirms that for many types of business it is an excellent location from which to serve the European market, and improved communications can do much to reduce such disadvantage as there is.

[29]   Treaty on European Union, Article 3 and Title XIV, Articles 130a to e.

But the range of economic activity that can operate successfully is inevitably narrower than in the more central regions of Europe.

Before discussing the role of policy measures, it is necessary to distinguish two separate aspects of the regional imbalance issue. The first is the effect on balance between Member States, since one of the consequences of EMU will be to make their economies more like regions of a single economy. Though retaining considerable discretion in fiscal policy, they will lose many of the present means by which they adjust their economies. They will continue to have more power of independent management than, for example, Scotland has within the United Kingdom, but substantially less than they have at the moment. This prompts the question whether regional problems might develop on a new scale, with the risk that whole countries turn into either prosperous or disadvantaged regions in the new Europe. The second issue is the effect of EMU on the existing disadvantaged regions, and whether it will make their problems easier or harder to solve. Not only are the present differences in income levels between Member States substantial, but the disparities between regions cover a much wider range.

Imbalances between Member States

The Adjustment Process

To understand what is at issue as the national economies of Europe increasingly acquire the characteristics of regions of the European economy, it is useful to start with a comparison of the means of economic adjustment available to nations on the one hand and to regions on the other. A separate national economy has at its disposal a wide range of macroeconomic instruments. These include: fiscal policy – alterations in taxation and public expenditure, with borrowing if necessary; monetary policy – the raising and lowering of interest rates and control of the money supply; and exchange rate policy – allowing the exchange rate for the currency to rise or fall. It should be emphasised that none of these measures involve a financial transfer from one country to another, except in so far as improving the competitive position in one country may worsen it in another, and hence raise unemployment there. Essentially such costs as the measures involve are borne by the country itself. In particular this is true of exchange rate adjustment, where devaluation only works if it succeeds in reducing the real living standards of those in employment to improve the market-ability of the output they produce. Restoring balance to the economy by these means may still be difficult and painful, as experience in Britain and many other countries has amply demonstrated, but the policy instruments have considerable power.

A typical regional economy does not have any of these instruments. Instead there is much greater capital and labour mobility between it and other regions of the national economy; this, together with a national structure of unions and employers' organisations and attitudes about equity in pay generally, are likely to produce wage and salary levels which are much closer to those in other parts of the country than would exist between separate states. The region is also likely, as part of a fiscal union, either to receive or contribute to budgetary transfers from richer to poorer areas. These raise living standards, increase demand and improve the quality of services in poorer regions, and may help to reduce inflationary pressure in richer regions in periods of boom. In addition there may be a regional development policy with measures specifically targeted at poorer regions or areas with high unemploy-ment. This would normally provide incentives to encourage investment in new productive capacity or pay for infrastructure as a means of improving the region's competitive position.

The range of measures typically applied to try to restore regional balance is therefore quite different from the macroeconomic measures used by national governments to restore inter-country balance. Which is likely to be more effective will depend upon individual circumstances. The smaller a country is and the more open its economy, the more difficult it is to pursue an independent macroeconomic policy, since the consequences for the balance of payments and the spill-over effects to other countries will be large. One of the consequences of increased European integration is that it has reduced the scope for independent action of this type by Member States of the Union. On the other hand regional development policy, although certainly assisting in ameliorat-ing regional problems, does not have a very good record in actually solving them. The fact that much the same areas in Britain have been scheduled as 'development areas' for most of the period since 1945 and even earlier gives striking evidence of this. This may be because regional incentives seldom have such a major effect in improving a region's competitive position as a devaluation does for a country, if, but only if, its effects in producing an alteration in unit costs can be made to last.

If one contrasts the European Union with the United States, the former being still a collection of nation states and the latter regions of a single economy, some interesting points emerge. First, there is very much more migration between the states of the United States than there is between European countries (and even two to three times as much as there is between regions within those countries). And secondly, disparities in income per head in the United States are far smaller than between the fifteen Member States of the European Union.[30] Over time there also appears to be a tendency for United States income differentials to narrow more obviously than in Europe, although the United States is not a country with a strong regional policy. It must be presumed that the high degree of factor mobility, both capital and labour, and institutional similarity across the whole country are of importance in explaining this. This shows that within a large currency union it is not inevitable that regional imbalances will worsen. Indeed it is by no means clear that if the individual states of the United States had freedom to conduct their own macroeconomic policies the imbalances would be less; and the general level of prosperity would be most unlikely to be so high.

The process of integration in which the European Union is engaged will take its Member States increasingly away from the national economy model and towards that of regions. The Single European Act has already provided for capital and labour mobility, although cultural and language differences will continue to make the latter much more immobile than in the United States for the foreseeable future. EMU will further increase capital mobility and remove some of the main instruments of macroeconomic policy from the national to the European level. As will be seen below there is a European regional development policy, though this is in supplement of national policies, and a European budget, but inter-country fiscal transfers are very small. Although the Union is gradually acquiring the characteristics of a single economy, it is likely to remain a long way short of the position of the United States or of any other federal country. The primary concern must therefore be that Member States should have adequate means to ensure the

---

[30]   Boltho, A, (1989), 'European and United States Regional Differentials: A Note', 5(2) *Oxford Review of Economic Policy*, pp 105–115; idem, (1992), '*On Regional Differentials between the United States and the EEC*', unpublished paper delivered to a CEPS conference, '*Economic and Social Cohesion in the EC*', 22–23 June, Brussels. Boltho argues that the comparative lack of mobility is partly responsible for the wider income differences in European states than in the USA.

adjustment of their economies to the differing circumstances that may affect them. Whether these are measures hitherto regarded as national macroeconomic policy, or increasingly those associated with regional adjustment, is of less concern than that they should be available and be effective. The danger lies in removing the power of national adjustment before anything adequate can be put in its place. Against this background the following pages examine the most likely causes of imbalance.

Potential Causes of Imbalance

The balance between two national economies or two parts of a single large economy may be upset by a wide variety of factors, some of which have been mentioned earlier in this paper. These include: different rates of inflation; external shocks, if these affect one economy more than another; different rates of productivity growth, if these alter the competitive position of some areas as compared with others; and population growth and migration, which affect the potential for economic growth and the pace at which new jobs have to be created if unemployment is to be avoided.

(a) Inflation

Of the possible causes of imbalance, the most likely, and probably most serious, is the persistence of differing rates of inflation. If this occurred, the country with the higher inflation rate would find that its goods became uncompetitive, growth stagnated, unemployment rose and its budget deficit increased. To some extent this situation will be self-correcting, as rising unemployment is likely to reduce the rate of inflation. But the process can be slow and painful: the economy suffers stagnation and in the meantime there is serious imbalance between the economies of Member States. As explained in part 1 of this paper, the resulting political pressures could put the whole future of EMU at risk.

This problem arises from a failure to achieve proper convergence. It may be that inflation rates in participating countries did not properly match each other in the first place or that they did at the time of entry to EMU but that for various institutional reasons – more militant trades unions in one country, greater structural mismatch in the labour force or less public fear of inflation – they no longer do. Whatever the cause one cannot expect fiscal transfers, regional policy or other EU cohesion measures to provide a solution to this problem. A failure of convergence cannot be patched up by subsidies from other Member States. If the root problem is not tackled, it may go on getting worse, so that the country becomes more and more uncompetitive. The only possible course, therefore, is to adopt fiscal measures to bring inflation down. If it has become an ingrained habit, as it has in many countries, the cost may be high in unemployment and loss of growth over what could be a long transition period. A country in this situation therefore faces a stark choice: either it joins EMU, imposing whatever measures are necessary to achieve convergence in the knowledge that there will be transitional costs; or it decides that this cost is too high and stays outside, running a more inflationary regime. While this latter course may be a softer option in the short term, it only makes sense if a country needs more time to bring its inflation down to levels that are compatible with convergence. For in the longer run it is unlikely to benefit from lower unemployment by staying out with a weak currency. As the experience of our own country in the 1970s and 1980s shows, inflation can become a habit with no lasting benefit to employment.

A rather similar problem would arise if, as a consequence of EMU, there were pressure to equalise earnings across participating countries, regardless of continuing differences in productivity. This is the situation that has arisen in the five east German *Länder* following economic, monetary and political reunification. The former East Germany faced acute economic difficulty in any event, because productivity was much lower than in West Germany and its markets in eastern and central Europe were disrupted. But, in addition, strong pressure to bring earnings closer to West German levels made it impossible for many of the region's businesses to compete in an enlarged Germany. Reunification was therefore followed by a dramatic fall in production – GDP in the eastern *Länder* in 1991 was only 55% of its 1989 level – and very high unemployment.[31]

The consequences would plainly have been disastrous, had it not been for huge financial transfers from West Germany, both to meet social security costs and to rebuild the economy. It can be argued that this situation occurred because, within what was seen as one nation, large differences in regional earnings were considered unacceptable; but the same sentiments made possible transfers amounting to 4.7% of West German GDP and as much as 44% of the GDP of the eastern *Länder*.

[31]   OECD, (1994 and earlier years), *Economic Surveys: Germany*, Paris.

If EMU were to lead to similar pressure across Member States for wage equalisation unsupported by increased productivity, the consequences would be disastrous, and it would be a grave mistake to proceed with the project at all. Unemployment would rise; and in the present political climate in Europe the richer countries would not be prepared to do for their poorer partners what West Germany has done for the eastern *Länder*. But, while admittedly a single currency will make it much easier to compare wage levels between countries, pressure for equality of earnings seems unlikely to be much more affected by EMU than by the Single Market. The tendency towards equality in wage and salary levels within nation states, which makes it difficult to adjust the competitive position of regions, is a consequence of national trades unions and employer organisations and established habits of comparability that follow from political more than from economic integration. These may become EU-wide features eventually, and if they do Europe's countries will indeed be more analogous to regions economically. Provision would then certainly have to be made for substantial inter-country fiscal transfers. Customs union, the Single Market and EMU may all prove to be steps in that direction, but such a situation is still a long way off. In the meantime, if wages levels do gradually converge, it seems reasonable to expect this to be based on improved productivity in the poorer countries as they catch up those that are more advanced.

(b) Growth of Productivity and of the Labour Force

Differing rates of growth in productivity between countries and of the labour force make possible, and indeed require, different rates of growth of GDP. Rates of growth of productivity do differ widely between the EU countries: Britain's growth of productivity in manufacturing has been faster than that of Germany or France since 1980, although the level of output per head in this sector is still lower;[32] and in Scotland the growth of productivity in manufacturing has been faster still, exceeding that of the United Kingdom as a whole over the last three decades (Table 1 over).

Growth of population, on the other hand, has been greater in most other European countries than in Britain in recent decades. In Germany and France this is partly a consequence of inward migration. In Ireland the rate of natural increase has been higher than in any other EU

[32]   *Competitiveness, etc*, op cit; Oulton (1994), op cit.

Table 1

Manufacturing Productivity Growth
Average annual % change

	1960-70	1970-80	1980-90
Scotland	4.1	2.0	5.2
UK	3.1	1.6	4.7
US	3.5	3.0	4.7
Japan	8.8	5.3	3.2
Germany (West)	4.1	2.9	2.3
France	4.5	3.2	3.1
Italy	6.2	2.5	2.9
Canada	3.4	3.0	2.8
Major 7 economies	4.4	3.2	3.5

Source: Scottish Office

country but so has the rate of net outward migration, with the result that the rate of growth of the labour force has been relatively modest.

A consequence of economic integration, and particularly EMU, is that the macroeconomic climate will become increasingly similar for all Member States. The relevant market for which business decisions are taken will more often be the European market, and it rather than that of the nation state will be seen as the home market. Producers, therefore, no matter what their country, will share the same market and will be affected by the same monetary and exchange rate policy. Within a single nation state these circumstances have tended to result in fairly similar growth rates across regions, even if resources are more plentiful in some regions and would permit higher growth there without causing inflation. In the United Kingdom, for example, the rate of growth of population in Northern Ireland is substantially higher than in other regions, so that even when economic growth there is at rates similar to the UK as a whole, unemployment remains a persistent feature of the province. In Scotland, although the rapid growth of productivity in manufacturing is very welcome, it also means that a faster growth of output would be necessary than in the rest of the UK if net emigration were to be reduced. Although Scotland's rate of economic growth has differed increasingly from that of the rest of the United Kingdom over the last decade, as a result of growing specialisation in North Sea oil activities and electronics, the principal influence remains the macro-economic climate created by Government policies for the United Kingdom as a whole. The economy therefore continues to grow at a rate which is insufficient to absorb the labour resources available.

There is a potential danger, therefore, that, if the macroeconomic climate becomes increasingly European rather than national, it will suit some countries and parts of countries much better than others. Some, such as the south of England, may find themselves subject to inflationary pressure with policies that are set to suit areas with faster growth potential; others may find that they cannot grow fast enough to absorb their labour resources. Traditionally this problem has been one of the principal justifications for regional policy. The only solution to this problem in the European Union, since regional policy on a scale likely to correct it is unlikely in the foreseeable future, is to retain sufficient flexibility in unit labour costs between countries to influence their respective competitive positions and growth potential. Precisely because inter-country migration is always likely to be much less than between states and regions in the United States, it is essential that differences in national and regional income levels remain wider than they are there, both to give those areas that need faster growth the competitive edge to achieve it and to provide rates of return that encourage investment.

(c) Asymmetric Shocks and Fiscal Transfers

External shocks are seen by many as one of the most likely causes of regional imbalance. Such shocks may affect some countries and not others, or they may affect them all but for institutional or other reasons the reactions may be stronger in some than in others. They may take place suddenly, as with a price rise for energy or raw materials, or they may be long term, as with the discovery of a new resource or the decline of an established major industry. Where the effect is favourable, it is likely to increase the prosperity of the country or region in relation to other parts of the Union; but it may also lead to a level of activity that causes inflation, and perhaps hastens the decline of less competitive activities. Where it is adverse, the effect will be deflationary and usually means that higher investment in the area is required to develop new forms of activity and make good the loss.

It was largely because of this problem that a European Commission working group chaired by Sir Donald MacDougall concluded in its report of 1977 that much greater provision for fiscal transfers within the EU was required before embarking on EMU.[33] Within a nation state, where the budget accounts for some 40% of GDP, a progressive system of taxation and public expenditure distributed in accordance with need provide an automatic system both of redistribution and stabilisation. Richer regions contribute more per head to the national exchequer than poorer ones; but the latter, especially if they have high unemployment, poor infrastructure and industries in need of support, get more per head in public expenditure. Within the United Kingdom, as a recent analysis has shown (Diagram 3), Northern Ireland, Wales, the Northern Region of England and Scotland all gain from this redistribution. The first three gain both because revenue per head is lower and public expenditure higher than the national average; in Scotland's case revenue per head is approximately equal to the average for the United Kingdom, but public expenditure per head is 17% above the United Kingdom average and 21% higher than in England.[34]

In federal states there are explicit mechanisms to provide for these transfers from richer to poorer parts of the federation. They may, as in Germany and Canada, be designed to bring the revenue of the poorer *Länder* or provinces closer to the national average; or they may be intended to ensure that expenditure is in accordance with need rather than local taxable capacity. The European budget is at present tiny in comparison with the resources available to the government of any federation – only 1.2% of European GDP compared with at least 20% for the upper tier of government in many federations and approximately twice this amount for the central government in unitary states – so that transfers on the scale that exists in either federal or unitary countries is clearly out of the question. And the present political climate in the principal net contributor countries, Germany and Britain, would make any substantial increase in the size of the European budget unlikely.

[33]   CEC (1977), *Report of the Study Group on the Role of Public Finance in European Integration* (MacDougall Report), Brussels. See also Sir Donald's article (1992), 'Economic and Monetary Union and the European Community Budget', *National Institute Economic Review*, no 140, pp 64–69; and Begg, I, and D Mayes (1991), *A New Strategy for Social and Economic Cohesion after 1992*, European Parliament, Research and Documentation Papers, Regional Policy and Transport Series No 1, Luxembourg.

[34]   The latest Scottish figures, which accord closely with those for Scotland in the diagram, are given in Scottish Office (1995), *Government Expenditure and Revenue in Scotland 1993–1994*, Glasgow: Economic Advice and Statistics Division.

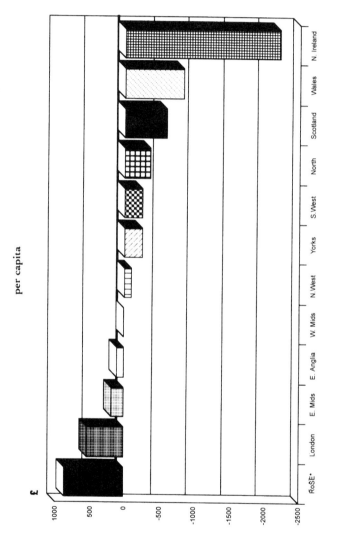

General Government Current Balance 1991

per capita

Note: The figures in this diagram relate to current expenditure only and do not include capital investment.
Source: Blake, N. (1995) 'The Regional Implications of Macroeconomic Policy', Oxford Review of Economic Policy, Vol II, No. 2.
* South East Region excluding London

Diagram 3:

These transfers fulfil two separate functions and it is essential to distinguish between them, if their significance for EMU is to be assessed.[35]

The first, and most widely recognised, is provision of comparable welfare services and basic infrastructure across the nation state as a whole. This is necessary for regional and social cohesion, because politically it is unacceptable within one country to have widely differing state pensions and unemployment benefit or health and education services. It may be that Europe will also one day reach a stage of political integration where such equalisation across the Union is considered to be necessary; and the process of closer economic integration, including EMU, may be a factor in bringing that day forward. But it would require much greater political solidarity than is likely in the foreseeable future and a scale of funding for the European budget that would permit transfers on a very large scale. In practice such developments would be impossible unless Europe acquired the main characteristics of a federal state.

The second function, and the one that has relevance to the problem of asymmetric shocks, is as an automatic stabiliser. Because so much public revenue and expenditure goes through the budget of central government in a typical nation state, expenditure varies with requirements and is unaffected by changes in locally raised tax revenue. Central government's freedom to borrow is also important, because even if increasing claims in some regions are not matched by higher tax revenue in others, the impact can be softened by varying the size of the government's deficit or surplus. The result of this is that the effects of a shock on a region, whether favourable or unfavourable, are reduced from what they would have been if either the region were wholly dependent on its own resources or the country lacked freedom to vary its borrowing.

There have been several studies of these effects. The MacDougall Report found in 1977 that the mechanism of central government funding reduced income disparities by 28% in the United States, 36% in Britain and as much as 54% in France.[36] The average for the five federal states studied (West Germany, Australia, Canada, the United States and Switzerland) was 35% and for the three unitary states (France, Italy

---

[35]   See CEC (1993), *Stable Money: Sound Finance*, a report of an independent group of economists under the chairmanship of H Reichenbach, published in *European Economy*, No 53, Brussels, pp 45–51.

[36]   CEC (1977), op cit.

and the United Kingdom) 46%. But this covered both redistribution and stabilisation effects.

The most recent study, by Bayoumi and Masson, separates the two.[37] It examined the United States and Canada, where there are substantial differences in the powers of federal and regional government. In Canada federal taxes only make up about half the percentage of income that they do in the United States; and Canadian provinces have more fiscal freedom, including borrowing powers, than their United States counterparts. Canada also has a more fully developed welfare system and, unlike the United States, the Canadian constitution gives the federal government a responsibility to provide 'equalisation transfers' to poorer provinces. The study found that redistribution flows amounted to 22 cents in the dollar for the United States and 39 cents for Canada; and that stabilisation flows were 30 cents in the dollar in the United States but only 17 cents in the dollar in Canada. Canadian provinces are therefore less cushioned against asymmetric stocks than the states of the United States, because of the smaller role of the Canadian federal budget in public finance, but redistribution is stronger, because of the higher level of welfare spending and the income equalisation objective.

In the European Union there is no 'fiscal federalism': slightly more than half the budget is spent on price support under the common agricultural policy, much of which goes to relatively prosperous areas, and only that part spent on the structural funds – currently less that 0.5% of European GDP – can properly be described as a transfer from richer to poorer areas. Even it is intended to be redistributive rather than providing stabilisation against shocks. But the same study found that national governments ensured, through their own budgets, stabilisation flows to the extent of about 31% of any change in income: this is therefore comparable to the United States and greater than in Canada. The authors therefore concluded that there did not appear to be a need for a major role in stabilisation at the European level, but only so long as national governments were able to continue to discharge this function.[38]

[37]   Bayoumi, T, and P R Masson (1994), *Fiscal Flows in the United States and Canada: Lessons for Monetary Union in Europe*, Discussion Paper No 1057, London: CEPR.

[38]   The Reichenbach Committee (CEC 1993, op cit) also takes the view that national measures to counter shocks should remain important, and that European measures in their support could be set up at fairly modest cost. They therefore do not support the scale of budgetary increase suggested in the MacDougall Report.

Clearly it is desirable for countries or regions to continue to be cushioned from the full effects of external shocks, although no system insulates them completely and it is a matter of judgement how far they should be protected. One suggestion, supported by the MacDougall Report, was for a European fund to support the unemployed, financed in part by employers' contributions across Europe as a whole. But so long as it is important for European countries to be able to maintain widely differing levels of real wages to maintain their competitive position, there would seem to be no case for anything like a Europe-wide system of comparable social security benefits. To attempt to create one would not only be impossibly expensive and politically unacceptable at present, it would also run the risk of producing pressure for higher wages in the poorer areas, since equalisation of benefits would unavoidably have repercussions on wage levels. This would have severely detrimental effects on employment if the resulting wage increases were not matched by productivity. But if Member States are to continue to operate their own fiscal stabilisation, there is a need for them to retain greater freedom of action in budgetary policy than can be exercised by any region or a state of a federation.

Where a shock affects a region or a part of a European country, it would be reasonable to expect that to be dealt with through the budget of the Member State, unless it is one of the poorer members. In that case the national effort may have to be augmented by special measures at the European level, including an increased claim on the structural funds. A shock that is so large that it affects a whole country, or the greater part of the country, is probably rare, but fluctuations which stem from the normal operation of the economic cycle can be more or less severe in some countries than in others; they can also, perhaps more importantly, be differently phased. An important recent study found that the core countries in the European Union – roughly those that would be most likely to participate in EMU from the start – were much less subject to being differentially affected by shocks than the remainder.[39]

In Britain's case this is borne out by experience of recent recessions and is not so surprising, given the stronger links that Britain still has with the North American economies than other EU members. In the European Union at present the option exists of letting the exchange rate

[39] Bayoumi, T, and B Eichengreen (1993), *Shocking Aspects of European Monetary Integration*, in Torres, F, and F Giavetti (eds), *Adjustment and Growth in the European Monetary Union*, Cambridge University Press for the Centre for Economic Policy Research.

take a large part of the strain if such shocks are substantial. Since that will no longer be possible after EMU, it is all the more important that Member States should retain sufficient headroom in their fiscal policies to vary borrowing. It could be disastrous if a rigid interpretation of the 3% deficit rule made this impossible. So long as the European Commission has no borrowing power and therefore contributes no fiscal element to macroeconomic management of the economy, it is essential that the Member States should retain the scope and the power to carry out this function.

(d) Asymmetric Shocks in Practice: Some Examples

The above paragraphs have set out the issues that have to be considered with regard to the problem of asymmetric shocks. But it helps to get the matter into perspective to consider what the effects might have been, had EMU existed when the two most obvious national scale shocks of the last twenty years took place: the development of North Sea oil and the reunification of Germany. Both show that it is a mistake to assume automatically that asymmetric shocks will be more difficult to handle within EMU than under present arrangements.

The discovery of North Sea oil had a major positive effect on the British economy but little or none on the other economies of the EU. In the development years of the 1970s the effect was massive capital investment, including a large inflow from abroad, and a boost to economic activity, especially in north-east Scotland. In the early 1980s, when production became substantial and the oil price was also very high, the impact was massive both on the Government's budget (up to £12 billion of tax revenue a year at peak) and on the balance of payments (approximately £30 billion).[40] Unlike the impact of direct capital investment, this fiscal effect was spread throughout the British economy. However, the oil price fell sharply from the middle of the decade and, although production reached a new peak in the early 1990s, the oil price remained low, with the result that tax revenues were £1–2 billion in the early 1990s on production valued at £8–10 billion.

In the first few years of the 1980s, coupled with tight monetary policies to control inflation, the sudden boost to the balance of payments caused a major surge in the value of the pound. From $1.60 in the late 1970s it reached $2.40 and DM 5 in 1981. It then declined to

[40] HM Treasury, *Financial Statement and Budget Report* (various years), London: HMSO.

fall below DM 3 by the end of the decade. It could be said that in this case the exchange rate took much of the effect of the shock, but the consequence was very difficult trading conditions for the rest of the economy. The recession of the early 1980s was accordingly magnified in Britain, with a drop of some 14% in manufacturing output between 1979 and 1981 and the largest rise in unemployment since the 1930s.[41]

Had EMU existed at this time and had Britain been a member, the budget would still have gained from the sudden rise in tax revenues, and the balance of payments effect would have caused an inflow of cash providing a stimulus to economic activity. But a single European currency, being more broadly based than the British pound, would have been much less affected. Had it risen at all against other major world currencies, such as the dollar, that would admittedly have been disadvantageous to the other European economies, but the effect would probably have been modest and could have been counteracted by appropriate policies. The recession would certainly have been less severe in Britain than it was. North Sea oil, both directly and through the budget, would have stimulated economic activity, and fiscal policies might have been necessary to control inflation, but the tragedy of North Sea oil squeezing out other tradable activities and, in effect, being used to finance unemployment could have been largely avoided.

The reunification of Germany involved political and monetary union between the two former German states. Apart from its particular implications for Germany, it gave rise to repercussions in the rest of the European Union. The rate at which the former East German currency was exchanged was widely considered by economists to be unrealistically high both for the effect it had on the competitive position of the East Germany economy and on accumulated East German savings. But of at least equal and probably greater importance was the leverage exerted by trades unions to raise wages in the east to something approaching levels in the west, as described earlier in this paper. The combination of these effects produced both a major boost to purchasing power and a catastrophic fall in production in the five eastern *Länder*, both of which caused an inflationary boom in West Germany. In the absence of an adequate fiscal response to control this pressure and with a revaluation of the D-mark against other European currencies ruled out as unacceptable, the Bundesbank raised interest rates substantially. But since the D-mark was the EU anchor currency, this

[41]   *Economic Trends* (1985), London: HMSO.

led other countries with weaker currencies to raise their interest rates to levels above those of the Bundesbank at the very time when they needed a monetary relaxation because of the recession. Apart from being a major cause of the destabilisation of the ERM, the result was a rise in European unemployment, considerably in excess of what might have occurred otherwise.

Had German reunification taken place after EMU, the effects would have been very different. The more fully Germany was integrated in the Single Market, the less the brunt of the demand effect would have been borne by West Germany and the more it would have spread to other countries. This itself would have lessened its harmful impact and benefited those economies in the recession of the early 1990s. Apart from that, since monetary policy would have been in the hands of the European Central Bank, the Germans would not have been able unilaterally to raise interest rates, with knock on effects throughout Europe. Either the demand impact would have had to be contained by a stronger German fiscal policy or it would have led to greater price increases in Germany and by that means spread to the other economies. Stronger fiscal measures would clearly have been preferable for Germany, since inflation, quite apart from the damage to Germany's reputation for price stability, would have amounted to a real appreciation, which would not easily be reversed when the need for it had passed. Sharper tax rises than actually occurred in the early 1990s would have been difficult politically, but if the Maastricht criteria were to be adhered to, there would have been little choice. Whichever course was adopted, the effect on the economies of the other EU countries would have been less damaging than the one actually followed.

These are but two examples of asymmetric shocks. It cannot always be assumed that they could be handled better within EMU than under present arrangements, and the potential for damage to inter-country and inter-regional balance needs to be recognised. The conclusion already reached therefore remains valid: that in the absence of a European dimension to fiscal policy, the importance of a continuing role for national policies to deal with shocks needs to be recognised. This certainly requires more flexibility than seems presently to be envisaged as well as a willingness to contemplate exceptional measures at the European level on the rare occasion when a really major shock affects one country.

The Effect on Existing Disadvantaged Regions

All countries of the European Union have some regions that are more prosperous than others. The problem of disadvantaged regions is, however, very unevenly spread: within the original six founder members of the European Economic Community regional problems were not a major issue except in Italy. There a large difference in living standards existed between the prosperous north and the much poorer south, including the islands of Sicily and Sardinia. In Germany, on the other hand, until reunification brought in the eastern *Länder*, the economy was regionally well balanced with smaller differentials than in the other large countries. But the enlargements of 1973 and of the 1980s made the Community less homogeneous, the economies of Ireland, Greece, Spain and Portugal being much less advanced than those of the existing members. Britain too, although comparable in living standards to the advanced economies of the original six members, had an interest in regional policy because of the need to introduce new activities in areas where old heavy industry was in decline.

Income levels now differ widely across the present Union of 15 countries. Diagram 4 shows that the poorest country, Greece, has a GDP per head that is less than half that of the richest, Luxembourg. The United Kingdom's GDP per head was approximately equal to the EU average in 1990, but in 1995 had fallen slightly below; Scotland's, at about 98% of the EU average in 1995, has improved slightly since 1990 and is approximately equal to the average for the United Kingdom. Ireland, Spain, Portugal and Greece, are significantly behind, although Ireland's position has improved considerably. Table 2 (over) shows the position in the richest and poorest regions in each Member State: the German city of Hamburg is at the head of the list with a GDP per head 184% of the EU average, and the Portugese region of Alentejo is the poorest at 35. In Germany, excluding the eastern *Länder*, the poorest region, Schleswig-Holstein, has a GDP per head almost equal to the Union average, while in Greece the richest, Attica, has barely half the average. In Scotland the Grampian region has a GDP per head 120% of the average and in the poorest, the Highlands and Islands, it is 78%.

European regional policy has been greatly developed since the first enlargement in 1973. The European Regional Development Fund (ERDF) was set up to finance infrastructure and industrial investment in designated qualifying areas, and in the 1980s this fund was brigaded together with the European Social Fund, which assists training and

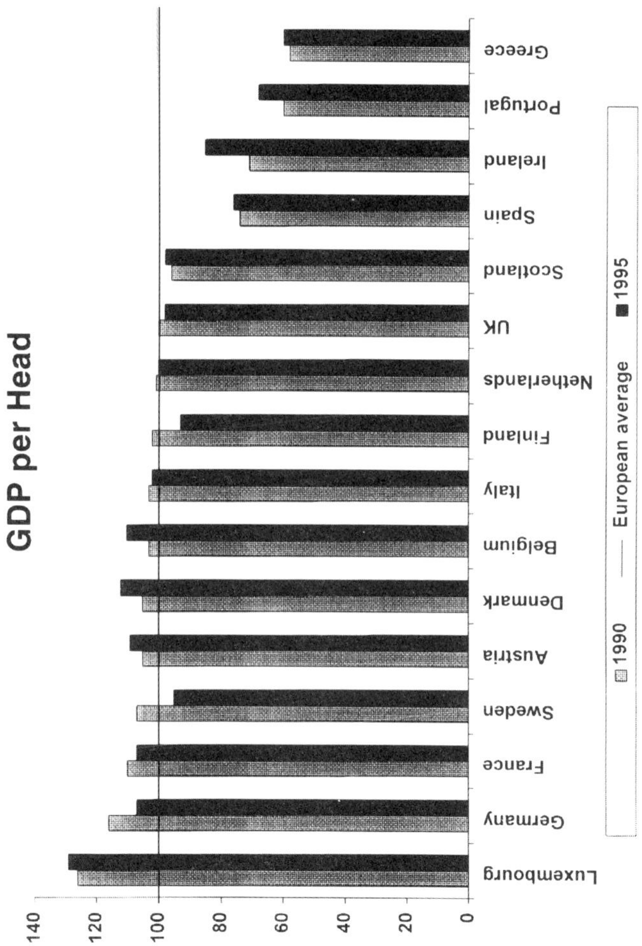
GDP per Head
140
120
100
80
60
40
20
0
Luxembourg
Germany
France
Sweden
Austria
Denmark
Belgium
Italy
Finland
Netherlands
UK
Scotland
Spain
Ireland
Portugal
Greece
1990
European average
1995

Source: European Economy and Scottish Economic Bulletin

Note: Scottish 1995 figure based on 1994 ratios.

German 1990 figure is West Germany only.

Diagram 4

Table 2

GDP per person 1990
Richest and Poorest Regions by Member State
EU12=100

	Richest		Poorest
Belgium			
Brussels	166	Hainaut	78
Denmark	107		
West Germany			
Hamburg	184	Schleswig Holstein	101
Greece			
Attica	50	Islands	45
Spain			
Madrid	96	South	59
France			
Ile de France	166	Corsica	79
Ireland	68		
Italy			
Lombardy	135	Calabria	61
Luxembourg	124		
Netherlands			
North Holland	118	Flevoland	61
Portugal			
Lisbon	76	Alentejo	35
United Kingdom			
South East	121	N. Ireland	74
Scotland			
Grampian	120	Highl'ds & Islands	78

Source: Eurostat Basic Statistics

retraining, and the guidance section of the European Agricultural Guidance and Guarantee Fund, which assists diversification in agricultural areas, to form the three structural funds. The activities of the three funds are co-ordinated to increase their effect on economic development and for the ERDF the territory of the European Union is divided into qualifying areas: those lagging regions suffering from underdevelopment (objective 1) being given the highest priority; regions with declining industry and in need of economic conversion (objective 2); and rural areas in need of economic diversification (objective 5b).

In 1988, at the time of the Single European Act and in recognition that it might have damaging effects on the weaker regions, a decision was taken to double the resources available to the structural funds by 1993. A fourth fund, the Financial Instrument for Fisheries Guidance, was added in the early 1990s to help areas affected by the decline in the fishing industry. The Maastricht Treaty also established the Cohesion Fund to contribute to projects in the fields of environment and trans-European networks, for which eligibility is limited to Member States with a per capita GNP of less than 90% of the average for the Union and which have a programme to enable them to meet the EMU convergence requirements – in effect Spain, Ireland, Portugal and Greece. Although the resources made available through these funds have greatly increased and now total ECU 24 billion a year, of which 85 per cent is spent on priority areas under objectives 1, 2, and 5b, they are provided to supplement existing national policies, which remain the main instrument for promotion of regional development. The last decade has, however, seen a substantial reduction in the resources devoted to national regional policies, notably in Britain, with the result that the relative importance of the of the European funds has increased.

The expenditure of the structural funds is spread widely across the European Union, but 80% of the total spent on qualifying areas is devoted to objective 1. Only Ireland, Portugal and Greece have the whole of their territory covered by objective 1, but a high proportion of Spain is covered and a large part of Italy. In the United Kingdom only Northern Ireland, and (since 1993) the Highlands and Islands of Scotland and Merseyside qualify under objective 1, but there is substantial coverage of objective 2, including much of Strathclyde, Fife and Dundee and some of objective 5b, including Dumfries and Galloway.

Disadvantaged regions are generally either too heavily dependent on primary activities (agriculture and fishing), or on older industries that are in decline (steel, shipbuilding, heavy engineering and textiles). In both cases employment is contracting. To absorb the surplus labour made available, they generally need a higher rate of economic growth than the rest of the economy of which they form a part. But their industrial structure, and in some cases their lack of infrastructure and their location, is likely to result in them having a lower rate. And even when their structure and location are not a handicap, the macro-economic climate, to which they are subject as part of a national economy, makes it difficult for them to achieve a rate of growth which is above that of the rest of the country. There is no simple solution to the problem. Improving the competitive position with investment in infrastructure, training and the attraction of inward investment are all important, but so too is the fostering of an entrepreneurial climate and the building up of a critical mass in key industries and services.

The Effects of EMU on Disadvantaged Regions

It is frequently assumed that EMU poses a threat to disadvantaged regions, and that because their economies are relatively weak they are likely to suffer more than they do at present. There are, however, potential benefits as well, and the balance is far from easy to predict. The experience of the 1980s, as Table 3 shows, was far from uniform among the regions, with some, such as Ireland and much of Spain, improving their position in relation to the rest of the Union, and others, mainly in Greece and the three regions in the south of Italy, losing ground. It is likely that such differences will continue with EMU, with some of the disadvantaged regions doing better and others worse than the average rate of economic growth in Europe.

However experience has shown that the disadvantaged regions taken as a group tend to improve their relative position when the European economy is enjoying rapid growth, and to remain static or lose ground when growth is slow. The Single Market was expected to contribute significantly to faster growth in Europe, and if EMU contributes to a fuller realisation of the benefits of the Single Market, it too may help to create a climate in which the disadvantaged areas can improve their position. On the other hand, if a disadvantaged region is part of a country which is having to impose deflationary measures in order to meet the EMU convergence criteria, growth is likely to be slow and unemployment high. In that situation it is not uncommon for the weaker regions to suffer most. While in reality this problem would arise

Table 3

The Performance of Objective 1 regions in the 1980s

Member State	Converging regions	Mixed evidence regions	Diverging regions
Italy	Abruzzi Molise	Puglia Sicilia Sardegna	Basilicata Campania Calabria
UK		N. Ireland	
Ireland	All regions		
Greece	E Macedonia Ionian Isles S. Aegean Isles Crete		C. Macedonia Attica Cent. Greece West Greece Epirus N. Aegean Isles W. Macedonia Thessalya Peleponnese
Spain	Andalucia Castilla La Mancha Murcia Canarias Valencia	Galicia Castilla Leon Extremadura	Asturias
Portugal	Lisboa Norte	Algarve Centro Alentejo	
France			Corsica

Source: European Commission (1995). *Cohesion and the Development Challenge Facing Lagging Regions*, Brussels

from inadequate national convergence rather than any problem within the region itself, it could result in a long period of deflation with damaging regional consequences.

The integration of the capital market will end exchange risk, and could be of major benefit to disadvantaged parts of the EU through increasing the flow of capital across national boundaries. Locations where production costs are low, because labour is readily available and economically priced in relation to productivity, and where land, factories and offices are cheap, could therefore attract substantial investment. There is already much cross frontier investment within the EU, but this could increase greatly with EMU, just as under the Gold Standard large amounts of capital flowed from London to other countries in the system. The outward flow from capital exporting countries at that time is estimated to have been as much as 5% of their GDP in 1913, an amount never equalled since.[42]

If this happens, an increased flow of capital from the more prosperous parts of Europe to the poorer areas could greatly help in improving their performance and reducing the present wide disparities in GDP per head. But such flows would only occur if costs in the poorer regions make them competitive and do not rise more rapidly towards those in the more prosperous areas than productivity.

The main risk of adverse effects arises from increased centralisation. The benefits of the Single Market were expected to come from increased competition, which in turn would lead to rationalisation and concentration of production in more specialised and more efficient units able to gain from scale economies. Improved productivity thus obtained would enable resources to be released and to be re-engaged in other productive activities. This was how the gains were to arise. Some of that rationalisation through increased competition is taking place, but, so far, the high levels of unemployment in Europe have prevented the redeployment of resources from being fully achieved. Even if it is achieved, the increased competition may cause large stronger units in prosperous areas to gain at the expense of weaker ones in disadvantaged areas, and especially those on the periphery; and the more economic growth takes place in central regions, the stronger this centralising tendency could become.

How likely is this to happen? It would be far too pessimistic to assume

[42] Panic (1992), op cit, pp 92–102; and Bairoch, P, (1976), *Commerce Extérieur et Développement Economique de l'Europe au XIX Siècle*, Paris: Ecole des Hautes Etudes en Sciences Sociales.

that peripheral regions will always have smaller and weaker production units than central regions and will inevitably lose out. But the example of Scotland shows that the number of major manufacturing firms operating internationally from a Scottish headquarters is small and tending to diminish. Inevitably the economy will have to rely more and more on branches and subsidiaries of firms that have their headquarters elsewhere, which will be sensitive to the economy's ability to continue to offer a competitive base for their operations. In addition the market is very imperfect when it comes to decisions about the location of investment. The costs on which entrepreneurs base their decisions seldom fully reflect the costs falling on society from their actions. The continuing growth of areas that are already suffering from congestion may result in high costs for investment in transport or other public services, or in inflationary pressure when labour or land become scarce. Areas where investment is inadequate to absorb the labour available suffer from unemployment and possibly a surplus of social capital. Firms that take location decisions may escape many of these costs, but all of them have to be borne in one way or another by society. This has always been the economic justification for state intervention in the form of regional policy.

For these reasons a strong regional policy in the European Union is certainly a necessity. The pattern of prosperous and disadvantaged regions may change and European economic integration is one of the factors that will cause it to change; but problems of regional imbalance are inseparable from a growing and changing economy. Frontier regions, for example between France and Belgium, which were on the periphery of their national economies, now find themselves in the centre of the Single Market. Parts of Spain, which offer low costs and an attractive environment, are already attracting investment rather as the sunbelt has in the United States. Ireland, despite a peripheral location, has attracted substantial international investment, and the same applies to Scotland. In a large market investment is free to go anywhere and non-economic factors such as political stability, the rule of law, absence of corruption and a welcoming environment can be at least as important as modest differences in costs. But in the end regional growth and prosperity depend on the ability to offer a location from which businesses can compete effectively with their rivals elsewhere in the Union. Economic integration, including EMU, increases the potential gain for disadvantaged areas, because businesses can now set up in Scotland, Ireland or Spain to serve Europe, which might never previously have considered the local or even the national market attractive. But the areas can also lose, because competition between locations for new investment is greatly intensified, and only those which can keep their costs down and maintain their attractiveness can succeed.

It is therefore impossible to predict whether EMU will reduce regional imbalances or make them worse. That depends on whether the advantages of increased market opportunities and better access to capital outweigh the tendencies to centralisation. The truth is that some regions will be able to take advantage of this situation and others may lose. And whether a region gains or loses will depend not only on what it can offer and its ability to seize an opportunity, but on whether the Member State of which it forms a part can adjust to membership of EMU without a painful deflationary transition. The role of regional policy, whether European or national, is to help the disadvantaged regions to strengthen their economies by enabling them to attract investment; and that role will be as necessary as ever, even if the regions which most require it gradually change. Regional policy is not a substitute for the automatic fiscal transfers in a nation state described earlier; it is directed at improving economic performance in a way that fiscal transfers are not. But its success is important to European integration and to EMU in particular, if it is accepted that in the end integration will only be politically acceptable if its benefits are widely spread. If the policy is not sufficiently strong, or if the measures fail, not only would the future of the Union be at risk but political pressure for more expensive transfers would become intense.

V Conclusion

Monetary union is a major issue for Europe. Arguably not since the Treaty of Rome itself have the Member States of the European Union embarked upon such an ambitious step. It is also high risk. If it fails, with the consequence that countries having joined are forced to leave it again, the cause of European integration will suffer an unprecedented setback. That could happen if countries join that are still dependent on a periodic devaluation fix to maintain their competitive position and before they are ready to abide by the disciplines of the common monetary policy. But if it succeeds, the adoption of the single currency will be a major landmark for Europe. It will give permanence and stability to the Single Market, give Europe a currency of truly world stature and enhance European prosperity.

In the long run the notion of a single market with fourteen separate currencies, each fluctuating and subject to speculative attack, is an absurdity. One has only to consider how strong the United States economy would be if it was split up into separate currency zones, or what the effect would be on business and investment in Scotland if the single market of the United Kingdom lacked the security of a single currency, so that the pound Scots was open to speculative attack and continually changing in value in relation to sterling. Sooner or later, therefore, the European Single Market needs a single currency if it is to deliver the benefits of integration that those who signed the Single European Act, including our own Government, wished to achieve. For this reason, if the present plan does not go through, a further attempt will have to be made later; or the D-mark will de facto become Europe's common currency with other curren-cies linked rigidly to it, rather as the Dutch guilder and Austrian schilling are linked to it today and as the Irish pound was linked to sterling for so many years. Such an arrangement would be a second best: it would put Europe's monetary policy in the hands of a single national central bank (as it largely is under present arrangements) and give other countries much less power to ensure that monetary decisions were taken in their common interest.

But to join a monetary union with economies that have not properly achieved convergence would be to court disaster. The Maastricht convergence criteria are crude and may be criticised in many respects, but it is essential that the participating countries should be able to live with similar rates of inflation without having to suffer lengthy stagnation. It is also necessary that participating countries should have their fiscal position under control. A union in which, say, one large country the size of Britain or Italy with about 15% of the population was allowed to run up a third of the total debt, would clearly be unacceptable.

But there is a serious danger in the rigidity of the intended fiscal arrangements and this could turn out to be a major shortcoming of EMU as presently proposed. Meeting the 3% budget deficit criterion is going to be difficult enough for aspiring participants, since so few of them meet it at present, and if the stagnation in the major Continental economies continues, it could become ever more elusive. In such circumstances attempts to meet it by yet further tightening fiscal policy could bring on another recession and make the prospect of meeting it even more remote. There is a risk, therefore, of compounding the present economic difficulties of slow growth and high unemployment. But the proposals are also unsatisfactory for the longer term management of the European economies. EMU could have brought the advantage of a much more effective macroeconomic policy than Member States can presently conduct individually; but there will be no European fiscal policy as a counterpart to monetary and exchange rate policy and no provision for borrowing at the EU level. It is therefore essential that the nation states should retain enough fiscal headroom to run their own counter-cyclical policies and to provide automatic stabilisers against shocks, as they do at present. To require them to live within the 3% deficit rule, regardless of the stage of the cycle or of any other circumstances, seems unrealistic, judging by the experience of the early 1990s; and to require those with deficits to pay fines, as the German Finance Minister has proposed, would only make matters worse. It would result in a fiscal policy which aggravated recessions instead of reducing their impact and could herald an era in which Europe had slain the inflationary dragon at the cost of semi-permanent unemployment and stagnation.

Monetary union will make participating economies more like regions of a single economy. But this is a matter of degree. They never enjoyed complete freedom of action and European integration has already increased interdependence. The participating economies in EMU will give up sovereignty over monetary and exchange rate policies; but by retaining control over fiscal policy (subject to the convergence criteria), they will avoid dependence for economic management on measures that have traditionally been regarded as regional policy, the position of Scotland within the United Kingdom. But if their budgets had to be more or less balanced, with much more restricted recourse to borrowing, as a strict interpretation of the Maastricht criteria might imply, a much stronger regional policy at European level and provision for substantial fiscal transfers would become essential. At present, and for the foreseeable future, there is not the political solidarity to make this possible.

The presently disadvantaged regions would be affected by monetary union if they found themselves part of a country that had failed adequately to achieve convergence and for that reason suffered a prolonged period of stagnation. The effects of this might fall disproportionately on the region, because disadvantaged regions often perform worse when national growth is poor. But the only solution to this is to ensure that convergence is properly achieved before joining EMU; it cannot be found in any kind of regional policy. EMU will also affect the regions insofar as it reinforces the rationalisation of production brought about by the Single Market. The expectation that this would lead to greater centralisation in Europe, with concentration on large production units in the central core of the Union, led the European Council to greatly increase resources available to the structural funds. But the truth is that there is no general rule for the effects on the regions. There are opportunities for gain as well as risk of loss, just as up to now some regions have improved their position in relation to the rest of Europe and others have fallen further behind. By removing exchange risk, EMU will increase the integration of the market and make the flow of capital across national frontiers easier. That means that a business in any part of Europe can be confident of access to the whole market on predictable terms. Regions with low costs but good infrastructure links will find their chances of attracting capital from high cost developed areas improved; and it is possible, as in the days of the Gold Standard, that there will be very substantial flows of private capital from richer to poorer areas. But the competition to attract capital investment will be intensified, and success will depend on ability to offer an environment in which that capital can earn a good rate of return. Some regions will benefit from this, and one can already predict areas of fast growth in the south of France and in Spain, where the gains are likely to outweigh any effect of centralisation. But others less well placed geographically, or where the political climate or other factors are less favourable could lose. Regional policy, both at national and European levels, will therefore remain a key priority to ensure that all parts of the Union are able to share in the benefits of increased prosperity.

For Britain a decision to exercise the opt-out from monetary union could prove to be a critical moment in its relationship with Europe. British experts and commentators have shown themselves more aware of the potential risks of monetary union than their counterparts in many of the other countries. It is right to be aware of the dangers, but there has also been much less recognition of the need for monetary union, especially the potential instability of the Single Market without a single currency. The Government has done little to put the positive case to the public. Instead the public, influenced by a succession of counterproposals and reservations – the 'hard ECU' proposal, the opt-out negotiations and the recent attempt to delay implementation – not surprisingly show little enthusiasm.

If the project fails, as it could, no doubt the Eurosceptics will say that it was inevitable. But if it goes ahead and succeeds, Britain has much to lose from standing aside. It would be a major mistake to suppose that little would be changed. There would be one currency for a population of perhaps 200 million people in Europe, with the likelihood that that number would increase. The Euro would inevitably dominate economic and monetary conditions in Europe for countries outside EMU as well as inside, to a much greater extent than the D-mark does today. Britain would have served notice that it preferred its independence, such as it was, to a place at the table where Europe's economic decisions will be taken; and at the world level the present Group of Seven leading economic powers might well give place to a Group of Three where the key decisions would be taken. The City of London, which is by far Europe's largest financial centre, was bound to lose out as a site for the Central Bank when the Maastricht opt-out was negotiated. A decision to exercise that opt-out will be a further important signal. While obviously London would deal in Euros, as it does now in Eurodollars, there would be many who would wonder if it were not sensible increasingly to base their financial business in Frankfurt. But perhaps the greatest danger of all would be for the opt-out to be read as a sign that

Britain was generally distancing itself from the European market; the potential loss of inward manufacturing investment could then be serious indeed, especially for Scotland.

And yet what can one expect a British government to do – even one more determinedly European than the present administration? One cannot escape the conclusion, as Mr Blair said in a recent speech in Japan, that the country is not ready either politically or economically to be a full member of EMU.[43]

Politically it is not ready, partly because the positive case has never been properly argued in this country, but also because of the searing experience of Britain's ERM fiasco. A commitment to enter EMU as a founding member would therefore be very controversial; it would be vigorously opposed by the Eurosceptics and by a substantial section of the press, for whom it would provide a cause to rally against. There would be high risks either that the project might fail or that Britain might fail to prosper within it. Critics would not hesitate to ascribe any failings in the country's economic performance to EMU participation. The problem is that the difficulties, if they arise, are likely to be short term and the benefits, though potentially substantial, would only be apparent in the long term. It is therefore hard to see any government taking the political risk of British entry in 1999. Nor is it clear that this would be right economically. Inflation, certainly, is now very low, but it is still above the levels in the best performing countries. Unemployment remains high, and we will only be sure that the inflationary danger is under control when unemployment is much lower than it is now. Economic growth has improved and the Chancellor expects it to be stronger in 1996 than 1995. But this has only been achieved with sterling's falling exchange rate against the D-mark. This option would be lost in EMU. Since Britain is not in the ERM and continues to depreciate, it does not meet at least one of the convergence conditions. It would be economically risky to enter EMU, even if the other members permitted it, without being sure that sufficient convergence had been attained.

But must one burn one's boats? Joining as a founder member or opting out completely are not the only choices. It may be that the most practical course would be for Britain to make it clear that it welcomes EMU for those countries that feel ready to participate in 1999, and that it expects to participate eventually but does not feel that adequate convergence is yet attained. Once the Euro has been introduced,

[43]   Reported in the *Financial Times*, 5 Jan 1996.

assuming it is indeed run as prudently as is presently intended, Britain should try to hold sterling steady to it in value, whether or not it participates in a formal ERM-type scheme, just as the Dutch and Austrians have held their currencies to the D-mark. To avoid speculative attacks this can be done without formal narrow bands. There would probably be a price to be paid for this in interest rates, which would be above those for the Euro, assuming the markets had greater confidence in the Euro than in sterling. But success would gradually narrow this gap, especially if the Government started to issue all or part of its debt in Euros rather than in sterling. Once it was clear, over say a period of five years, that sterling could maintain a constant value to the Euro without damage to the economy, full participation in EMU would no longer be any more risky than monetary union between the Netherlands, Austria and Germany would be now. The advantage of this course is that it would be an approach to EMU by stages: it would allow the Continental countries that feel ready to adopt the 'big bang' that they prefer and at the same time allow the cautious British to adopt a gradualist approach, which is much more likely to succeed for this country in the end. For Britain the Euro would first become a common reserve currency before becoming the single currency. This would have some similarities to the Treasury's own 'hard ECU' scheme and to some of the other schemes for quasi-monetary union that have been put forward in the past. It would reduce the obvious dangers of loss that Britain is likely to face if it simply opts out of EMU indefinitely, and it would also enable progress towards full participation to be taken at a pace that would be politically and economically practical.

Appendix A

**Government budgetary positions
(as percentage of GDP)**

| | General government net lending (+) / net borrowing (-) | | | |
	1990	1993	1995	1996[a]
Belgium	-5.8	-6.7	-4.1	-3.3
Denmark	-1.5	-4.5	-1.6	-1.4
Germany[b]	-2.1	-3.5	-3.5	-4.0
Greece	-14.0	-12.1	-9.1	-7.9
Spain	-4.1	-7.5	-6.6	-4.4
France	-1.6	-6.1	-4.8	-4.0
Ireland	-2.3	-2.4	-2.0	-1.6
Italy	-10.0	-9.6	-7.1	-6.6
Luxembourg	4.9	1.8	1.5	0.9
Netherlands	-5.1	-3.2	-4.0	-2.6
Austria	-2.2	-4.1	-5.9	-4.3
Portugal	-5.5	-7.1	-5.1	-4.0
Finland	5.4	-8.0	-5.2	-3.3
Sweden	4.2	-13.4	-8.1	-3.9
UK	-1.5	-7.8	-9.8	-4.6
EU-15	-3.5	-6.3	-5.0	-4.4

Source: European Commission 1996

[a]European Commission Projections

[b]Western Germany up to 1990, unified Germany thereafter.

[c]General government gross debt figures are not adjusted for the assets held by the Danish Social Pension Fund against sectors outside general government and for government deposits at the central bank for the management of foreign exchange reserves.

| | General government gross debt | | | |
	1990	1993	1995	1996[a]
Belgium	130.9	137.5	133.7	130.6
Denmark[c]	59.6	80.3	71.9	70.2
Germany[b]	43.8	48.2	58.1	60.8
Greece	82.6	114.5	111.8	110.6
Spain	45.1	60.4	65.7	67.8
France	35.4	45.3	52.8	56.4
Ireland	96.5	97.4	81.6	74.7
Italy	97.9	119.4	124.9	123.4
Luxembourg	4.6	6.3	6.0	7.8
Netherlands	78.8	81.3	79.7	78.7
Austria	58.3	63.0	69.0	71.7
Portugal	68.6	67.2	71.7	71.7
Finland	14.5	57.3	59.2	61.3
Sweden	43.5	76.2	78.7	78.7
UK	35.3	48.6	54.1	56.3
EU-15	55.1	66.2	71.3	73.5

Source: European Commission 1996

[a]European Commission Projections

[b]Western Germany up to 1990, unified Germany thereafter.

[c]General government gross debt figures are not adjusted for the assets held by the Danish Social Pension Fund against sectors outside general government and for government deposits at the central bank for the management of foreign exchange reserves.

Appendix B

List of Abbreviations

CEC	Commission of the European Communities
CEPR	Centre for Economic Policy Research
CEPS	Centre for European Policy Studies
ECB	European Central Bank
ECU	European Currency Unit
EMI	European Monetary Institute
EMU	Economic and Monetary Union
ERM	Exchange Rate Mechanism
EU	European Union
GDP	Gross Domestic Product
GNP	Gross National Product

PART 2
The Impact of Monetary Union on Regional Economic Imbalances

VI A European Perspective

Bruce Millan

Introduction

I am speaking as a politician, not an economist. Gavin McCrone's paper has set out the economic issues very fairly; but EMU has an important political motivation as well and it is with that that I would like to start. Of course there has always been a political objective in the moves towards integration right from the start of the European Economic Community, though there has never been complete consensus over the form it should take. This is not just a problem that affects the United Kingdom, although it is manifested more seriously and more openly here.

If one considers the agenda for the forthcoming Inter-Governmental Conference (IGC), it is difficult to see how agreement can be reached on any substantial issue. The Westendorp report demonstrated that there were serious differences of view between Member States. There is also, although perhaps not quite so openly, some disagreement on the question of enlargement to eastern and central Europe. I therefore propose to extend my consideration of the issues, in a way that they rarely are, to the prospects for EMU in a union of not fifteen but perhaps twenty-five members.

The decision has already been taken to offer countries in eastern and central Europe, not to mention Cyprus and Malta, full membership of the Union. This has been repeatedly reiterated by heads of government at their six-monthly summits, most recently at Madrid in December 1995; but there is a tendency for heads of government to make grand statements and leave the problems to other people. The real problems that this proposed enlargement raises have not been properly addressed so far. Yet negotiations, at least for the membership of Cyprus and Malta, are expected to start within six months from the end of IGC; and there seems to be a growing commitment to start negotiations with other applicant Member States soon thereafter.

Sir Edward Heath has drawn attention to his reservations about offering full EU membership to the countries of central and eastern Europe, rather than some form of closer association. He is the first substantial political figure I have noticed to have done so, and he can hardly be accused of being among the Euro-sceptics. But the negotiations are to begin, and in view of the state of these countries' economies, I expect them to involve, whatever the timetable, extremely difficult decisions. We are therefore considering EMU against this uncertain background – the question of enlargement on the one hand and a lesser degree of consensus among existing Member States about the future of the union than for a considerable time.

Maastricht and the Popular Mood

We need to be aware of the difficulties that this will raise. Events following the Maastricht Treaty demonstrated the dangers of taking too much for granted in assuming the support of the Union's citizens for major change. This illustrates the importance of bringing the Union nearer to the citizens, an issue which is meant to be addressed at the IGC. The negative vote in the first Danish referendum on the Maastricht Treaty and the French referendum, which was a close run thing, almost killed off Maastricht completely, and, looking at the most recent entrants, it is doubtful if the Swedes, the Finns and the Austrians would now vote so strongly in favour of their countries' participation as they did in 1994.

This more sceptical position arises not least, I think, because of Europe's serious unemployment problem. It is difficult to persuade people of the benefits of union when there are nearly 20 million unemployed. They are liable to ask what the Union is doing about this critical situation, and why unemployment is not among the criteria for EMU convergence. Indeed it is not even mentioned in the Treaty, although the Swedes are seeking to get an employment chapter inserted. All of this affects the public perception of the Union in a very damaging way.

Divided Views over EMU

The controversy over EMU is not only to be found among the public at large; in the United Kingdom it also divides businessmen. A recent CBI survey showed quite a narrow majority among members for participating in the first stage; there was a considerable percentage against and a large number undecided. This division not only applies to businessmen but even to bankers. In Germany too it is a divisive issue, partly in consequence of the widespread attachment to the Deutschmark. The German Social Democrats have adopted a more sceptical tone in recent months and the new leader of the party, Mr Lafontaine, has made some critical speeches. In France we have seen the violent· reaction which the Government's austerity programme provoked, a programme of cuts which was intended to help France achieve the convergence criteria laid down for EMU. So even in the two countries where there is the strongest political will to achieve the EMU, there are difficulties in persuading public opinion of its advantages.

The Convergence Criteria

These problems have prompted discussion both about whether the convergence criteria need to be maintained in their present strict form, and whether it is necessary to stick to the proposed timetable. But the latter was confirmed at Madrid and there is no prospect that the IGC will change or revise the conditions on convergence set out in the Treaty, especially as Treaty changes require unanimity.

The criteria for convergence do, however, allow for some flexibility in their application. If this is stretched too far, it would of course make a nonsense of having such criteria. As yet there has been no sign of this; but the fact is, that on a strict interpretation of the 1995 figures for inflation, budget deficit and government debt, only Luxembourg would qualify for EMU. This position will probably change before early 1998 when decisions have to be taken; but even if some flexibility of inter- pretation is applied, only a comparatively small number of members states are likely to qualify. And although there is much talk about increasing convergence, the 1995 situation was worse, not better than 1990, as the figures in Diagram 2 of Gavin McCrone's paper clearly demonstrate. If therefore EMU proceeds with only a comparatively small number of members, it must inevitably lead to a multi-speed, two-tier European Union.

A Two-Tier Union

In fact, the Maastricht Treaty for the first time made a two-tier Union possible. Previous Treaty changes were made on the basis that all countries had the same objectives and intended to move forward together or, if they did not, it was only because some required time to catch up. Under the Maastricht Treaty it has been made possible for Member States to opt out not only from EMU, but also from the Social Protocol, even in circumstances where they adequately meet the conditions for participation. We can expect this kind of provision now to be extended to other areas, such as foreign policy. I believe that this has considerable implications for the character and future management of the Union of a kind which have hardly been considered so far.

The Regional Impact of EMU

Under full EMU, with Member States all operating a single currency, their economies effectively become regions of a single economy. This has major implications for economic management and particularly the balance between the economies of Member States. The issues are perhaps most evident in relation to the four countries that qualify for assistance from the Cohesion Fund, and I should like to start with them. This fund was provided for in the Maastricht Treaty to give additional assistance to the poorer countries in the Union. These were defined, quite arbitrarily, as countries that had GDP per head of less than 90% of the Union average: Greece, Portugal, Ireland and Spain.

If we take **Greece** first, the latest figures that I have, as published by Eurostat, show that in 1993 the GDP per head in Greece was 63% of the Community average. It has been stable, or stagnant to use a more pejorative term, for a number of years. Greece does not meet any of the convergence criteria at the moment and does not expect to meet them in the short term, though the formal Government policy is to work towards them.

Spain is rather more prosperous. GDP per head was 78% of the Community average in 1993, taking the country as a whole. However it has a number of very poor regions and, as well as not meeting any of the convergence criteria,[1] it has an unemployment rate – the highest in the Community – of 22%. I must say that to introduce an austerity

[1] Apart from membership of the Exchange Rate Mechanism (ed).

programme with its deflationary and employment effects in that situation does not make the slightest bit of sense to me. Yet Spain is politically committed to being among the first members of EMU, even although it is very unlikely that it will be. In any case it not only does not make sense economically for Spain to follow a deflationary programme, but it is also very doubtful how far it will be publicly acceptable. The previous socialist Government had serious problems with the trade unions and others, and Mr Aznar, who is now in the process of putting together a centre-right government, is likely to face similar discontent.

Portugal is very much concerned with what happens with Spain and is always anxious that Spain does not move ahead of it in Community terms. Portugal does not fulfil any of the criteria at present but again has a declared Government policy of entering the EMU at an early date, if not among the first members.[2]

Portugese business, I see from a recent report, has however appealed to the Government not to try to join before Spain and Italy, Portugal's major trading partners. They are worried about competitive devaluation. Portugal's GDP per head was 69% of the Community average in 1993. I have seen a recent report from the Union Bank of Switzerland that its current position may have deteriorated because of the attempts to meet the convergence criteria. Whether or not that is accurate, I must say again that any deflationary policy in Portugal would not make sense to me. I would also add what may sound a technical point about the use of the Community's Structural Funds in Portugal, but which is in fact rather important. When I negotiated with Portugal in 1989 for the use of the Structural Funds for the first period for which I was responsible, the maximum rate of assistance available for programmes was 75%. However Portugal decided not to apply the maximum rate but use rates of, say, 50 or 60% so that they could spread the funds more widely over their economic development needs. In the negotiation for the present period, which runs from 1994 to 1999, Portugal asked for the maximum rate because of a much tighter budgetary position, associated with the attempt to meet the Maastricht criteria. So we now have the position in Portugal – and it applies elsewhere – that although the total funds have been increased the impact is not being properly realised, because it is being spread over a narrower base.

In the case of **Ireland** the GDP per head in 1993 was 81% of the

---

2 Portugal, like Spain, is a member of the Exchange Rate Mechanism (ed).

Community average, which incidentally is well beyond the 75% threshold for the so called Objective 1 status presently enjoyed by Ireland. I should say that Ireland is the Member State which has been most generously treated by the Structural Funds, with an assistance per head of population well above what we are giving to Greece and Portugal, both considerably poorer countries. It is an anomalous position but it will continue until 1999, and it has been part of the reason why the Irish economy has had the highest growth rates in the Union in recent years, though there is still a serious unemployment problem. Ireland meets the economic convergence criteria except for the level of Government debt, but that is reducing and there is a fair prospect that, with the necessary degree of flexibility, Ireland would be taken as qualifying for the first wave of entry to EMU.

Leaving Ireland aside for the moment and considering the other poorer Member States more generally, even if they did manage to meet the criteria for entry to EMU, what happens if any or all of them are unable to sustain that position? Indeed what happens to any Member State in that position? There are of course provisions in the Treaty, to take effect in the third stage of EMU, for various penalties and fines. But I am sceptical as to whether it would ever be possible to implement these provisions. The political damage would be immense. First of all, you have to identify publicly a member which is failing to meet its obligations: that is a political decision of quite exceptional difficulty. And then there has to be agreement on the penalties to be imposed. Obtaining such agreement would raise all sorts of problems.

Incidentally it is seldom realised that there is already provision for penalties in the legislation on the Cohesion Fund. The regulation governing the fund states that if adequate steps are not being taken by a Member State to deal with an excessive deficit, payments from the Fund can be suspended. This is perverse because it means that when one of the Union's poorest countries is already facing difficulties financially, you make matters worse by taking European money away from them. So far such action has not been implemented but the possibility illustrates the problems.

In any case, given the divergent levels of prosperity among Member States in the present Community and the difficulties of sustaining convergence, it is unrealistic to envisage the EMU covering all the existing Member States within any credible timescale.

The Single Market

In my view that disposes of the argument, which has been frequently advanced, that EMU is essential for the operation of the Single Market. Obviously it cannot be essential, because the Single Market is operating at the moment, yet only a minority of Member States are going to be in EMU. It is certainly desirable that there should be exchange rate stability, but it cannot be argued that a single currency is absolutely essential. This becomes even more apparent if it is related to enlargement. The average GDP per head within the central European countries is only about 30% of the Community average and in the case of Romania and Lithuania it is even less, around 20%. If they join, these countries will be expected to meet the rules of the Single Market to the letter, and not just to the letter but to a very considerable number of letters. Last May's White Paper from the European Commission, describing the things they had to do, runs to 430 pages and sets out a formidable agenda for them. What is perfectly clear is that, even if they do join the Single Market, they could not on a sustainable basis meet the convergence criteria for monetary union; that is why some are now looking some twenty years ahead for participating in EMU. This reinforces my view that exchange rate stability is desirable, but EMU is not indispensable to the working of the Single Market.

Fiscal Transfers

Differences in living standards within the present European Union, not to mention the situation that might arise after enlargement, raise the question of fiscal transfers. Here, I do not think that it is transfers to deal with asymmetrical shocks that raise the greatest problem. A Member State that gets into difficulty can be given temporary help, but where there are real differences in GDP per head and in the ability to meet the convergence standards, there are more permanent difficulties. The MacDougall Report of 1977, which studied such transfers between regions in both federal and unitary states, suggested that, for EMU to succeed, significant transfers from richer to poorer Member States would be necessary, much larger than existed then or have existed since.[3] And it should be remembered that, at the time of the

---

[3]   CEC (1977), *Report of the Study Group on the Role of Public Finance in European Integration* (MacDougall Report), Brussels.

MacDougall report, there were only nine Member States with much smaller differences in living standards than exist now after the enlargement of the Union to include the three Member States from southern Europe.

The general feeling now seems to be that Sir Donald MacDougall exaggerated the scale of what would be required; but that may be no more than a rationalisation based on present circumstances. The fact is simply that the political will does not exist to provide transfers of resources to poorer Member States and regions on the scale that he argued for. The present budget of the European Union amounts to no more than 1.2% of European GDP, still only a fraction of what he proposed to make substantial transfers possible. Yet the present allocations to the Structural Funds are almost certainly more generous than would be agreed if the negotiations were taking place today. The key decisions were taken at the Edinburgh summit in 1992 and the budgetary period for the structural funds runs to 1999. The British Government was perhaps more willing to contemplate a generous settlement at that summit, when they held the presidency and were fearful that the summit would collapse in disarray if agreement was not reached, than they would have been since; and the position of other countries, notably Germany and Netherlands, has also hardened.

If the European Union is to succeed, countries must accept that there have to be net contributors as well as net beneficiaries; the Union cannot be succesfully run if no country is prepared to make a net contribution. Yet at present virtually every country is seeking to minimise its contribution and maximise its benefit. It used to be suggested that the Member States who have just joined would have an idealism which was lacking in the older members and, in particular, that the relatively wealthy Scandinavians would be prepared to contribute substantially more than they took out. In fact my experience of the negotiations on the Structural Funds was that these countries were anxious to get as much as possible from the Funds and were also very much aware of their overall budgetary position. The result is that, although Sweden and Austria do make net contributions, they are small countries and the contributions are not very large; Finland is a net recipient of funds.

There is no great pool of potential money, therefore, and there is already talk of the present arrangements for the Structural Funds being changed, to make them less generous even to existing Member States, when they are revised in 1999. The one certain thing is that these Funds are not going to be extended on the present basis to new applicant countries, because the budget could not afford it, or, more accurately, nobody is willing to pay the bill. The Union will therefore be refusing to take the steps necessary even to make it a possibility that all Member States in an enlarged Community can become members of EMU.

If one accepts that EMU is not going to apply to all members, there will be difficult problems of exchange rate relationship between those countries that are in and those that are out. It is not yet clear how this is going to be settled. Mr Tietmeyer of the Bundesbank has suggested that the proposed European Central Bank should not only determine monetary policy for those who are members of EMU but should also determine exchange rate policy for those EU members that remain outside. That seems to me unlikely to be acceptable, to put it mildly, especially as a principal reason for remaining outside EMU is to retain freedom to adjust exchange rates. But nobody else has come up so far with an alternative that is likely to be generally acceptable.

In any case the Maastricht provisions for EMU involve a transfer of economic and monetary decision making from national governments to a central authority that is much more far reaching than anything else in Maastricht, or indeed anything else in the Treaty so far. For the poorer Member States I have already said that it does not make sense to me for them to put themselves under the rigours of EMU, to pursue deflationary policies or to forego the possibility of devaluation. Even for the more prosperous Member States the question of devaluation is not irrelevant, as the United Kingdom's experience since our exit from the ERM in 1992 testifies.

Given the significant loss of national decision-making involved in EMU, the benefits would have to be correspondingly substantial and as little subject to uncertainty as we could make them.

The Position of the United Kingdom

Coming now to the United Kingdom's position, I do not think that there is a distinction to be drawn between the effect of EMU on the United Kingdom as a whole and on the British regions. If EMU is good for the United Kingdom, it will also be good for the regions, so long as the Government has an effective regional policy in operation, an assumption which has not always been valid. It is also, of course, necessary that there will be continuing support for our disadvantaged regions from the European Union. There is about £1.5 billion each year coming to the United Kingdom from the European Structural Funds and this will continue throughout the current financial period to 1999.

The scale of the Structural Funds is not always appreciated. Everyone knows that the common agricultural policy is expensive. But expenditure on the CAP is reducing as a percentage of the total Community budget, so that it will take no more than 43% of the budget in 1999. At the same time expenditure on the Structural Funds will have expanded to 35%. The gap is therefore narrowing and the budget for the Structural Funds is already substantial. The greatest danger to the continuation of this funding to the regions comes not so much from EMU as from the extra burden of financing enlargement, since it may be that the additional costs of including central and eastern European countries in the Union will be met by reducing expenditure in present Member States. Similarly an increasing proportion of Europe's private investment could be diverted to the east. The consequences of enlargement are therefore likely to be much more substantial in the end for the United Kingdom regions than those which would follow from EMU. In the debate about EMU in a country like the United Kingdom, the regional effects are not the major issue.

The Major Issue

The major issue is that it is clear that, despite current embarrassments about even the Germans failing to meet the convergence criteria, the French and the Germans are determined to press ahead; and if they are determined it will happen. We are under an illusion if we think it will not happen, simply because the technical provisions have not been met. There has always been a danger in the United Kingdom that we have underestimated the political will to integration.

So I think EMU is likely to happen and probably on the existing timetable. That being so, I think it would be completely irresponsible to say that we will not join under any circumstances. That is quite absurd. The decisions, in any case, do not have to be made for another couple of years. But equally I do not think there is either a sufficiently strong economic case at the moment, or the kind of political atmosphere in the United Kingdom, in which a decision to join in 1999 is likely to be taken, either by the present Government or any succeeding

Labour Government, even if the United Kingdom qualified for entry then.

It is not normally in my nature not to be firmly on one side or the other on this kind of issue, and I dislike therefore having to say 'let's wait and see' before finally making up our minds. However in the present political situation in the United Kingdom I think it is sensible to keep our options open.

The logic of that position means not only rejecting the view that we should not join EMU whatever the circumstances. It also means rejecting the contrary argument that, if EMU does go ahead, then we *must* join and that it would be an absolute disaster if we were not among the first entrants. That again is a matter for judgement at the time. I say that being well aware that on European issues the United Kingdom has been too often too reluctant and too late.

I say it too as a committed European and one who deplores the antics of the so-called Euro-sceptics, whose aim is essentially to take us out of Europe altogether. Nor do I wish to see the United Kingdom isolated in Europe, as on so many issues we already are: that is not in our interest. But I do not think the test of being a good European should rest on one's view about EMU. There are lots of other issues and the present Government has done tremendous damage to the British case on so many of them by choosing to adopt a general Euro-sceptic attitude either out of conviction or because it has allowed itself to be pushed in that direction by what is still a minority within its ranks. We must not always look at things as if the rest of the Community is looking for opportunities to do us down. It is not like that: Member States try to be helpful to each other at Council meetings and to reach agreements which are acceptable to all, even when only a qualified majority decision is required.

Finally, as I said at the beginning, I have been speaking as a politician. I have also been speaking personally. The views that I have expressed this morning are exactly the same views as I had when I was a member of the European Commission, though you must not take them as being representative of the Commission's views then or now. They were my views then. I expressed them in the Commission at the time, and they are my views now.

Discussion following Bruce Millan's paper

It was argued in discussion that the financial markets were now increasingly expecting EMU to go ahead and to start more or less on schedule. This was shown by the convergence of long term bond rates in the countries most likely to be members. On that basis it was possible to predict that Germany, France, the three Benelux countries and Austria would be among the founder members. But some of these countries, notably France and possibly even Germany, would have difficulty in meeting the 3 per cent criterion for budget deficit. The start of EMU would therefore depend on the political will to make it succeed rather than a precise meeting of the deficit criteria. But if it was admitted that countries with budget deficits up to, say, 4 per cent of GDP might join, a significant chance arose that Spain, Portugal and Sweden could be admitted. Finland and Ireland were already well placed to meet the criteria. If that were to happen, and it seemed increasingly a possibility, EMU, far from being confined to a small group of countries, would be very large, embracing perhaps 11 countries and a population of some 250 million.

Britain would then find that a large and important financial market, comparable with the dollar market, had grown up of which it was not a member. That market would be looking for top quality securities; and bonds placed on that market would be well received internationally. It would therefore attract funds even from countries that were not members of EMU. Preparations for EMU were much more advanced on the Continent than many people in Britain seemed to realise, even to the extent of multinational companies speaking of paying their employees in Euros as early as 1999. If Britain ignored these developments, it would do so at its peril.

Against this it was argued that if EMU was to succeed it should start with a small group of countries with economies that were broadly similar and therefore responded in the same way to the economic cycle and to external shocks. To widen it to include other countries was to court disaster, because the mechanisms were not in place to make adjustment possible. The resources were not available to provide fiscal transfers on a scale that would ensure social stability in such a system. The total spent on the Structural Funds amounted to less than 0.75 per cent of European GDP. It had been said that monetary union did not necessarily require political union; but the scale of transfers from rich areas to poor that would be necessary to make the union work might only be possible with some form of political union.

Turning to the position of the United Kingdom, it was pointed out that in the timing of the economic cycle the British economy is not synchronised with the economies of Continental Europe. In the 1990s it experienced the onset of recession earlier and has been recovering while they are relatively stagnant. Because of the very different state of the financial markets, notably the prevalence of short-term rather than long-term debt and the use of variable interest loans, for example in housing, the response of the economy to interest rate movements was also very different from other countries. For these reasons it would be difficult for the United Kingdom to be part of a monetary union where monetary policy was set to meet the needs of the other countries.

Turning to the regional issue, Bruce Millan's view was questioned that if EMU was good for countries it was likely also to be good for regions. Against this it was argued that the effort to comply with the convergence criteria, notably a tightening of fiscal policy, was likely to depress economic activity in several countries and the increase in unemployment could impact disproportionately on the weaker regions. It was also possible that cuts in public expenditure to meet the criteria could result in substantial reductions in the funds available for regional policy. On the other hand better control of inflation and reduction of public debt could have a positive effect on regional development, as could easier movement of both capital and labour across national boundaries. What was needed was an adequate system of support measures for the regions both at the European and national levels.

Finally, it was pointed out that for Britain the important issue was not whether or not EMU should go ahead. Britain had its opt-out and could not expect to have much influence on that decision. The issue for Britain should be what it should do if EMU did go ahead as seemed increasingly likely in 1999. If Britain was outside there were two possible dangers. One was that interest rates might be significantly higher than in the EMU core group, because sterling might be seen to be at greater risk of depreciation and less credible monetary policies. The second danger applied particularly in Scotland where inward investment from abroad had become so important to the economy. If it was seen that the United Kingdom, lacking a constructive engagement in Europe and a stable currency relationship with EMU, was in danger of losing its unfettered access to the Single Market, the damage to the economy from the withdrawal of these companies could be very serious. While the conclusion in Gavin McCrone's position paper was accepted, there-fore, that the United Kingdom was neither ready politically nor economically to participate in EMU at the outset, a debate was badly needed on Britain's relationship with the EMU countries. It was essen-tial to establish a framework for monetary and exchange rate policies that would minimise the dangers of being outside.

VII A German View

Norbert Walter

Background

My paper is not balanced and does not claim to be scholarly, nor is it representative of a German view. It is very personal, but I hope that from a statement of my personal position you will be able to gain some useful insights as to how others in Europe see the prospects for EMU.

I was born at the end of the war. My two grandfathers both died in 1916 at Verdun; in the Second World War my father fought both against the French and the Russians. But I was lucky: I was born into a Europe that was already becoming integrated, that was more and more open; and it gave us freedom, openness and open-mindedness. It gave us the chance to increase our wealth through division of labour to an extent that our Continent had never before experienced.

My views are based on beliefs that are founded on the Catholic religion; I also believe that there should be limits to government and that government should be in accordance with the principle of subsidiarity. We have had the benefit of the protective American umbrella and this, combined with integration, an open society and limited government, has given us a long period of peace and prosperity. Unfortunately, we are beginning to take this for granted, and we therefore do not appreciate what we have to do to preserve this integration process with all the benefits it has given us, for our children and our grandchildren.

I believe Europe has been failing exactly when it should have been the star of the 1990s. The peaceful revolution that overcame communism offered the possibility of an even wider division of labour within Europe, a prospect that I am sure Adam Smith, who lived and worked in this city, would have applauded; he would have understood the need to develop our institutions to seize that opportunity. But instead we have been content to be observers. German reunification was a major event which created an asymmetric shock of the kind already referred to at this Colloquium. It had implications not only for Germany but for Europe; but where were the other Europeans to help the Germans make unification a success? We mismanaged unification, and our European friends could have helped to dissuade us from the costly social policies and over-regulated approach that we adopted. We might then have spent less money in a way that has done little good; and interest rates would not have had to be raised so high. Unification would thereby have been less of a burden for Europe as a whole. But lack of interest on the part of Europe has applied not only to the challenge facing Germany; it is the same with Italy. When they tried to overcome the Mafia, when they sought a better electoral system, we were content to remain observers and complain about the inability of the Italians to achieve political stability.

When Helmut Kohl said of EMU that Europe had either to carry on with the process of integration to ensure peace or to drift back to fragmentation and hostility, his remarks were not well received in the United Kingdom. But I have deep respect for what he said. The real monster is not the Maastricht Treaty, it is non-Maastricht. We cannot stand still, we have to carry the process of integration forward and extend it to Central Europe as well. If we debate whether Prague or Warsaw belong to Europe, or whether enlargement is timely or whether we can afford it, we are standing in the way of history. The Czech Republic was always part of Europe. These countries were taken away from us by communism and now they are back. They share our values: they have established a democratic system and the market economy, and we neither can nor should tell them to stay out of the European Union. If we insist that we cannot, or cannot afford, either to widen or to deepen the integration of the Union, I believe we will miss an historic opportunity.

Convergence

Immediately after the signing of the Maastricht Treaty, the main concern was whether there would be sufficient price stability in Europe to make possible a coming together of rates of inflation. Now, out of the four convergence criteria, three are practically fulfilled by all of the Member States that can be considered serious candidates for EMU.

There is acceptance across Europe of the need for price stability and the measures necessary to secure it; and the financial markets reflect this, with the result that long term interest rates are closer together than might have been expected at the beginning of the 1990s, when the criteria were agreed. It is also understood that we cannot continue to use adjustments in exchange rates as an instrument of economic management. Even countries that wish to retain nominal exchange rate adjustment as a policy measure of last resort recognise that rates cannot be changed unilaterally and that stability in exchange rates is essential for a truly functioning internal market.

The only criterion which is not adequately met is fiscal convergence. Here we all have something to learn from the Irish case, where a sound and courageous fiscal policy has resulted in a substantial reduction in outstanding debt. In most countries both public expenditure and tax rates are too high, with the result that our productive resources – both entrepreneurs and employees – are driven out of the official economy either into the shadow economy or into other countries. We therefore need to reduce government intervention, whether it is in the form of taxation to pay for redistribution or to provide subsidies to sectors that are weak and unlikely to perform adequately in the future. In practically every country we need to reform our public welfare system. If we do not do these things, we will not have a sustainable fiscal policy. If the Maastricht convergence process pushes us into making these reforms, that will be a benefit. But there are dangers if the criteria are interpreted too mechanically: the nature of budget deficits needs to be carefully analysed, so that we understand better how far they are structural, and therefore a long term problem, and how far they are cyclical and self-liquidating as economic activity recovers.

Monetary Union and Political Union

It has been argued that monetary union necessitates political union. While in general I accept this, anyone who has seriously thought about the matter ought to accept that the European Single Market also necessitates a measure of political union; and the advantages of the Single Market have been accepted by everyone. If we are not to have internal borders, it is meaningless to pursue separate national migration policies. It is inconsistent to open our frontiers to the flow not only of goods and services but of capital and persons, yet keeping migration policy under national control. There ought to be a common European migration policy. There also ought to be a common policy for internal security and some form of common approach in foreign policy and defence. So it is not just monetary union that requires some element of political union: in adopting the Single Market we have already taken a step that requires a common political approach in a variety of different areas.

Regional Imbalances

In observing regional differences I always ask myself whether we are really looking at disequilibria, or whether such differences are simply a form of market stability. If people do not emigrate out of a region that has consistently lower income towards those where it is higher there must be a reason behind it, and the same applies for regions with high unemployment. In more cases than we perhaps suppose, these differences reflect equilibria rather than disequilibria, and a regional policy that attempts to overcome them is therefore bound to fail. As Harry Johnson, the well-known Canadian economist, used to say, 'water finally runs downhill'. I think this may be true of attempts to correct regional differences. What we need to do is to give equal opportunity to individuals, so far as we can, rather than concentrating on results as measured by statistical disparities.

The Need for Stable Money

One of the presidents of our Central Bank once said that the Euro is the money you cannot print. That is to say governments cannot print it to pay for their indebtedness, because the supply is not under their control. The question is, therefore, do we want our politicians to have a say in the pursuit of monetary policy or not? Much may depend on how we view monetary policy, but the experience of the 1970s and 1980s shows that money illusion is fading and with it the benefits of exchange rate adjustment. The little benefit that can be got in temporary increases to output and employment has been declining, and the high costs of unstable money and inflation, which are increased by variable exchange rates, are better understood. In such circumstances it should be widely accepted that any institutional change that gets responsibility for money creation out of the hands of those who are engaged in the political process is a good thing. That is not to say that a central bank will be intelligent enough always to pursue appropriate policies. I have myself criticised the Bundesbank in the past. I know that everything is easier with the benefit of hindsight, but I would still argue that the Bundesbank has made a number of mistakes in its monetary policy. Nevertheless I do believe its status as an independent institution is the reason why it has not made as many mistakes as other central banks. It is obvious, however, that Germany's European partners cannot be deprived of their own monetary sovereignty by indefinitely tying their policies to those of the Bundesbank. The Bundesbank is managed by a German board and its statutes require it to frame its policies with regard to economic conditions in Germany, not in Europe. What is needed is a central bank for Europe as a whole, which, in setting its policies, takes account of European conditions and in the management of which all countries that belong to EMU have influence. But the principles which underlie the operation of the Bundesbank could and should be copied for this new European institution. The statutes of the proposed European Central Bank give good reason to believe that a sound monetary policy would be followed, and that not only Europe but the international community would have a currency that would be considered both valuable and stable.

Currency stability has a space dimension as well. If there is a single currency across what are at present different currency areas in Europe, it would no longer be necessary for a firm to ensure against exchange risk by having at the same time separate industrial capacity in, for example, Northern Italy and Southern Bavaria. There would no longer be the danger that, because of no more than exchange rate fluctuations, one location in Europe is more competitive for production this year and another next. So the rationalisation of production will save capital, and there will be greater stability in levels of regional economic activity as well.

That is not to say that I expect a single currency and monetary stability to eliminate unemployment, neither do I think that the present unemployment is a consequence of too strict a monetary policy. I think that most of our unemployment stems from attitudes that were quite understandable in the 1960s and early 1970s, but that we now have to reform our social policies and our subsidies if it is to be reduced. Europe is not rich enough to support the number of unemployed that we presently have, but to reduce it we must pay less in subsidies to uneconomic industries and reduce transfers to resources that are idle.

Free Trade

I want to conclude with some comments on European integration and free trade. There are those who think it is not important to have a common currency but who nevertheless still believe in the importance of free trade and the free movement of capital and labour. Yet the lesson of history is that free trade can only be sustained if some world superpower is prepared to take the initiative in promoting it and underpins it with other policies. That was how it operated under the leadership of the United Kingdom in the last century, and in this century that role has been played in part by the United States. The alternative is to create some supranational institution with the means to enforce such a policy; and this, I believe, is what we have in Europe.

But we need constantly to build on this approach and to enhance its political legitimation. This means not only that the European Parliament needs to be more deeply rooted in the electoral process but that we have to think ahead to the future. In a generation's time the government of Europe cannot be carried out by the present style of European Commission; it will have to be undertaken by a body that reflects more directly the impact of the election process.

I will end by reminding you of what Churchill said in his famous speech in Zurich in 1946. He urged those Europeans who were politically and economically ready and who were willing to embark upon European solutions to pull ahead and set an example for the others.

Discussion following Norbert Walter's paper

It was suggested by one speaker at the start of the discussion that the United Kingdom's opt-out from the Social Chapter in the Maastricht Treaty was more damaging to the European Union than its opt-out from EMU. Picking up Dr Walter's comments, he emphasised that there was a need for a debate on the lack of flexibility in European labour markets and on the extent of labour market regulation. This debate had ceased as soon as it was clear that the United Kingdom, the main proponent of flexibility, was not going to participate.

So far as EMU was concerned, the Maastricht Treaty was sometimes portrayed as damaging to employment; but in reality monetary discipline that led to low interest rates and low inflation was good for growth and good for employment, as the Bundesbank's example in Germany over many years had shown. Several speakers argued that budgetary discipline was a necessity in any event, with or without the Maastricht Treaty.

It was pointed out that the United States provided an example of an economy where monetary policy, as managed by the Federal Reserve, was much more independent of Government than in most European countries, but individual states retained considerable scope to vary fiscal policy.

Referring again to the situation in the United States, it was pointed out that there were extremely large flows of population movement from one state to another. This was how job opportunities in the American economy were matched with labour resources. Since, after EMU, it would no longer be possible to use monetary and exchange rate policies to bring about adjustment between the economies of European Member States, it was argued that large flows of labour from one country to another would be necessary in Europe too, if serious problems of unemployment were to be avoided. Yet Europe was a very long way from achieving inter-country movement of labour and population on anything like the American scale.

Referring to Dr Walter's remark about the level of public debt in Ireland, a speaker from Belgium, where gross government debt was the highest in the European Union, argued that a high debt country could not realistically be expected to comply with the reference value of 60% before entry to EMU. A simple arithmetical example would have shown that, even with sound fiscal policies, debt could not be reduced quickly to the reference value, and that for such an adjustment ten or fifteen years would be a more realistic timescale than three years.

In summing up, Dr Walter said that the American perspective on many of these issues was helpful. The European Union would of course have a very small budget compared with the Federal Government in the United States, and in that respect it is not comparable. But the United States showed that it was possible to have a single monetary policy coupled with diversity in fiscal policy; and it also showed how important it was to have a flexible labour market and flexibility in prices as well as wages. As regards the timing of EMU, he believed that if Europe missed its opportunity now, it would be a generation at least before monetary union could be on the agenda again. But his guess was that it would go ahead, if not exactly on time, at least very soon thereafter.

VIII European Monetary Union and Regional Policy

Carlo Santini

Introduction

In presenting my paper I propose to draw on the experience of Italy, since, in my opinion, Italy more than any other member of the European Union exhibits dualism between its regions.[1] This dualism is acute and apparently intractable. The rapid approach of the date for the European Council's decision on the transition to the third stage of Economic and Monetary Union and the impending introduction of the single currency have fuelled a vigorous debate throughout the Continent.

High unemployment and the cyclical slow-down in Europe have strengthened the position of the opponents of Maastricht, who argue that these evils are rooted in the Treaty itself and in the deflationary policies necessitated by the convergence criteria. Conditions of slow growth and high unemployment aggravate the problems of the less advanced areas. There can be no surprise at the liveliness of the debate over these choices, which will be of historic importance for our Continent. What is perhaps surprising is the time it has taken, at least in some countries, for the debate to get underway.

Italy has acute problems of public finance, inflation above the European average and a severe economic dualism. Progress has been made on several fronts, but not enough; in the last few years the gap between North and South has actually widened. In addition dramatic political

[1] The author wishes to thank Mrs P Caselli and S Chiri, who have assisted him in preparing this paper. F Papadia and S. Rossi have read a first draft and provided useful comments. The author remains, however, solely responsible for the text; moreover the opinions expressed do not necessarily coincide with those of the Bank of Italy.

crises have, for many years now, deprived the country of stable and effective leadership and created uncertainty over the continuity and effectiveness of policies of adjustment.

Some of these general themes will be touched on in the concluding section of my paper, but the main focus of the paper is on regional disparities and regional policies in Italy and in Europe. I start by presenting some of the data illustrating the extent of economic dualism; I then trace the main stages in the development of the Community's regional policy; and, finally, I will offer some reflections on the possible impact for the less advanced areas and for regional policy of the transition to a single currency.

The Case of the Italian Mezzogiorno

The North-South Gap

The Mezzogiorno comprises six regions located to the south of a line across the Italian peninsula from Rome to Ancona, plus the two major islands of Sicily and Sardinia. It accounts for about a third of the Italian population. Measured by the standard yardsticks of per capita GDP and unemployment rates, the conditions of the region are comparable to those of the least advanced parts of Europe, while those same indicators show the rest of Italy to be among the most prosperous parts of the entire Community. Since the second half of the 1980s, moreover, the Mezzogiorno has been the least dynamic area in the Community.[2]

In view of the economic disparity between the two parts of the country and comparatively large size of the South, it comes as no surprise that Italy has long been the member country allocating the highest proportion of its GDP to public spending on regional development.

The present disparities between South and North are summed up in Table 1. Per capita GDP in the Mezzogiorno is less than 60% of that in the rest of Italy. Only 28 of every 100 persons are employed, as against 40 in the North. As regards structure, industrial employment plays a relatively minor part in the Southern economy and food remains a more important element in consumption than in more prosperous areas. The

[2] Commission of the European Communities (1994), *Fifth Annual Report on the Socioeconomic Situation and the Development of the Regions of the Community,* Brussels.

Table 1

ITALY: NORTH – SOUTH GAP (1994)

	South	North
Per capita GNP (thousand lire)	19.682	33.812
Participation rate	35.1	43.0
Unemployment rate	19.2	7.6
Net imports as per cent of GNP	14.7	– 8.7
Employment (shares):		
- agriculture	5.6	2.7
- industry	21.3	32.3
- services	73.1	65.0
Household consumption (shares):		
- food	22.0	17.1
- other goods	36.9	36.2
- services	41.1	46.6

Sources: Istat, Svimez.

Table 2

INFRASTRUCTURES GAP
(Italy =100)

Infrastructures	NORTH		SOUTH	
	1992	1987	1992	1987
Economic	**117.0**	**122.9**	**67.8**	**60.9**
Transport	107.9	109.2	87.8	85.1
Communications	117.3	118.3	69.5	68.1
Energy	113.6	127.2	75.3	60.6
Water	130.6	133.8	46.0	39.4
Social	**115.2**	**118.5**	**70.2**	**72.2**
Education	100.6	109.0	99.0	87.4
Health care	107.2	109.5	87.2	83.1
Sport	120.7	123.6	63.4	57.0
Civic	129.1	156.9	48.8	36.1
Cultural	120.5	120.3	63.8	63.8
TOTAL	**116.0**	**120.4**	**69.1**	**67.0**

Sources: Confindustria – Ecoter (1990); Del Castello (1994).

competitive disadvantage of the South, which is highlighted by the region's substantial trade deficit, is related in part to its poor infrastructure, which is estimated to be only 60% of the provision in the North (Table 2).

The enormous differences in economic structure, productivity, em-

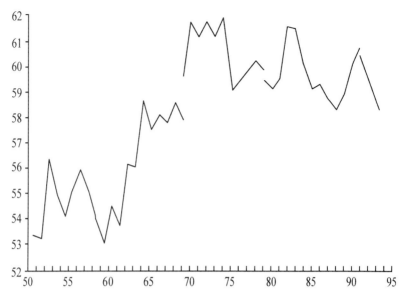

Figure 1. North-South Gap (ratio of per capita income in the South and in the North)
Sources: Istat, Svimez

ployment rates and the endowment of social capital civic traditions, are the sources of a centuries-old geographical dualism.[3]

In the past half-century, notwithstanding ambitious and costly programmes of economic integration and development, the disparity was reduced significantly only during the 1950s and 1960s (Figure 1). This was because between 1958 and 1963, the years of the Italian economic miracle, a million southerners found jobs in the north; a determined industrial development policy giving priority to public and private investment was adopted; and there were continuing benefits from actions taken in the 1950s, notably on land reform and new transport infrastructure. However the oil shocks of the 1970s handicapped the energy-intensive heavy industries that public corporations had established in the south; labour emigration dwindled to a trickle; public intervention grew less generous and, what is more important, less efficient.[4]

The inefficient use of public resources by the regional authorities

[3] Putnam, P. (1993). *Making Democracy Work: Civic Traditons in Modern Italy*, Princeton: Princeton University Press.
[4] Even regardless of the oil shocks, the long-run wisdom of decisions resulting in the concentration of capital-intensive investment in a region of abundant labour like the south of Italy was questionable.

began and there was an increase in social disorder.[5] The spread of organised crime was fuelled in part by the emergence of an acute employment crisis.

As measured by per capita GDP, economic conditions in the Mezzogiorno today are comparable to those of the rest of Italy in 1972. But some regions in the South, such as Abruzzi, Apulia and parts of Sardinia, have begun to display considerable economic dynamism. What is more, the progress gained in the 1960s demonstrates that the proper combination of forces can make inroads against the backwardness of the South. Policies based on such a combination must be resolutely pursued, especially in view of the constraints and the opportunities of the Single Market and the EMU. A renewed extra effort is needed, founded not only on increased Italian and European financial resources, but on a redesigned development policy, more efficient administration by the local authorities and the co-operation of business and labour.

National Policy and Regional Equalisation Today

The national interest in winning the regions of the Mezzogiorno back to the process of economic development is perhaps keener today than ever for a variety of reasons: the South is an important market for domestic output; the whole country's economic potential would be increased by higher employment in the south; both social stability and Italy's international role would be enhanced if the threat of continuing crises in such a large part of the country were removed; the drain on national resources which threatens to undermine the national budget would be removed; and even monetary policy would become easier to operate with a better balanced national economy. Italy therefore needs to come closer to its full potential output, which is now far greater than that actually achieved, owing to the severe underutilisation of human capital. Italy also needs microeconomic regional development policies that enhance the flexibility of the labour market, both as regards wages and labour utilisation.

Italy's southern development policy has now been radically over-hauled to enhance its economic rationale. It has embarked on a path marked out by five complementary guidelines, each representing a break with the past:

[5] Helliwell, J. F. and P. Putnam (1995), *Economic Growth and Social Capital in Italy*, Eastern Economic Journal, Vol. 21, No.3.

(1) Full compliance with the fundamental rules for EMU. The amount of grants, their administration and the areas covered are now adapted to the eligibility requirements for Community co-financing; and grants are not given, without special authorisation, if they conflict with European Union competition policy.

(2) Greater emphasis on public investment in human capital and productive infrastructure.

(3) Recognition of the shortcomings of the regional governments' implementation of development policy and the launching of remedial measures.

(4) The termination of the reductions in the social contributions paid by employers in the South, which have formed a sort of trade barrier protecting southern products. This change has made it all the more urgent to increase regional labour market flexibility to offset lower productivity and thus create a propitious environment for private investment.

(5) Greater reliance on business and labour organisations, to give them responsibility to draw up local pacts to foster the more flexible use of labour and wage differentiation between companies, and to encourage the establishment of new complex production facilities.

The aim all these lines of action have in common is limiting state interference in the workings of the market while making the most of its development potential, and instead focusing public action on the supply of essential public goods, on infrastructure, and on support for more flexible industrial relations.

Territorial Disparities in Europe and Community Regional Policy

The Mezzogiorno is undeniably a special case with its own particular features. But the persistence of the regional disparities in per capita output, in human and material capital, in technology and in the level and distribution of affluence is a phenomenon that Italy shares with a good number of other EU members. And, as in Italy, in some countries the disparities have worsened in recent years. In a number of countries there is a growing uneasiness with regional, national and community policies that have failed to achieve any appreciable, lasting reduction of the disparities between the economically advanced and less developed or declining areas.

At the European level, both the enlargement of the Community and German unification have amplified regional disparities within the Union and at the same time sharpened competition for the scanty funds available for regional programmes. The prospects of further enlargement to include countries in central and eastern Europe and the Mediterranean can only make these problems more compelling and more intractable. What is worse, the full implementation of the Single Market and the resulting increase in competition could aggravate the difficulties of the backward areas, at least during the transitional phase. How to solve these problems and prevent further decline is the fundamental issue for future regional policy.[6]

In embryonic form European regional policy started with the formation of the European Community itself. But even after the creation of the European Regional Development Fund, following the entry of Britain and Ireland, and a number of other reforms, it is fair to say that until the end of the 1980s regional policy was never underpinned by a proper strategy.

The foundations of a real regional policy for the Community were laid by the reform of the Structural Funds in 1988. This reform substantially increased the size of the Funds (doubling their resources in real terms between 1987 and 1993), tightened co-ordination between them and designed a system of forward planning of interventions. It also established six common objectives on the basis of which funds are allocated to individual projects, not, as was done previously, according to fixed quotas for each country.[7]

The regional policy guidelines established by the 1988 reform can be summed up as follows: concentration of intervention in the areas where it is most needed, selected according to a set of economic, social and demographic indicators; close co-operation between national and Community authorities; careful planning of expenditure over the medium term; and a stipulation that Community funding be in addition to national programmes.

[6] Padoa-Schioppa, T. (1987), *Efficiency, Stability and Equity,* Oxford University Press; De la Dehesa, G. and P. Krugman (1992), *EMU and the Regions,* Occasional paper No. 39, Washington: Group of Thirty; Armstrong, H., J. Taylor and A. Williams (1994), *Regional Policy* in Artis and Lee (eds) *The Economics of the European Union,* Oxford University Press.

[7] The six objectives are: the development of backward regions; the conversion of declining industrial regions; the integration of the long-term unemployed and youth into the labour market; vocational retraining; conversion of agricultural structures and rural development; the development of underpopulated regions.

Let me dwell at slightly greater length on the second of these guidelines – co-operation between the national and Community authorities. This co-operation responds to two needs: first, it makes up for the lack of Union presence at local level; and second it conforms with the principle of subsidiarity enshrined in the Maastricht Treaty (Article 3b). In practice, close co-operation has meant the delegation of virtually all responsibility to the national authorities, especially for project execution.

The suspicion that, once appropriated, the funds may escape the control of Community organs has been one of the grounds for the stiff resistance of net contributor countries to the expansion of the Community budget; and one can hardly help sharing this concern. Devising more stringent forms of control to govern the use of the Structural Funds is consequently a highly relevant consideration, if Union regional policy is to gain increased resources as well as improving in effectiveness.

The latest reform of the Structural Funds, in 1993, was enacted in response to fears that pursuit of the convergence criteria for the third stage of EMU might place an excessive burden on the backward and least prosperous regions. As in 1988, the Funds' resources were substantially increased. Revision of the Common Agricultural Policy is to reduce the scale of the Agricultural Guidance and Guarantee Fund as a proportion of the total Structural Funds as well as drastically reducing farm price support in favour of agricultural conversion and adaptation. A new Structural Fund was established to help adaptation and modernisation in the fisheries industry,[8] and the Cohesion Fund was set up, as provided for in the Treaty of Maastricht, to assist the integration into EMU of the four countries with low per capita income (Portugal, Spain, Ireland and Greece). Nevertheless, with the prospect of further enlargement to include countries of eastern and central Europe and the Mediterranean, the size of the Union's budget will remain a key issue.

Assessing the adequacy of the resources earmarked for the European Union's regional policy is not an easy task. Although the increases in the Structural Funds in 1988 and 1993 are substantial and are expected to bring the total provision for the Funds to 0.5% of the European Union's aggregate GDP by 1999, this still appears inadequate in relation to the severity and complexity of Member States' regional disparities. However, measured against the GDP of areas that are

[8]   The Financial Instrument for Fisheries Guidance (FIFG)

potential beneficiaries, these Funds are quite substantial. In addition, and particularly in the light of the Italian experience, there is a great deal of room for improving the efficiency with which the Funds are utilised and this must be done before any request for additional resources is made.

Regional Disparities and Policies with a View to EMU

The debate on regional disparities and on policies for overcoming them has taken on a new dimension in the light of EMU and especially the proposed single currency. The question is whether there is adequate wage and price flexibility, labour mobility and appropriate redistributive mechanisms for dealing with the regional impact of shocks to enable it to succeed. Many of those who have voiced scepticism about EMU have noted that Europe hardly meets these conditions (in particular the EU budget remains very small). As a consequence, they argue that the loss of the exchange rate as a tool for stabilisation will result in an excessive burden, especially for the more backward areas. Let me suggest three counterarguments.

First of all, the theory of optimum currency areas, so widely cited, is inspired chiefly by the American experience. But the United States as a currency area has much sharper regional differences in economic structure than those between member countries of the European Union.[9] It follows that severe asymmetric shocks are less likely in Europe. What is more, in the last few years, the social partners, in Italy as elsewhere, have displayed greater acceptance of wage flexibility and labour mobility as strategic elements in the battle against extensive mass unemployment.

Second, EMU will bring benefits that the theory of optimum currency areas fails to take into account, such as the gain in credibility from being part of a financially stable area, which is potentially greater for the more backward countries. This should result in lower inflation and lower interest rates – in short, an economic environment more conducive to investment and growth. While some people have argued that disparities in living standards have widened between Member States in the last few decades, it is not clear, even if it is true, that this should lead to rejection of EMU. The benefit of retaining the exchange rate as an

[9] See Helg, R., P. Manasse, D. Monacelli and R. Rovelli (1994), *How Much Symmetry in Europe*, CEPR working paper.

adjustment mechanism may well be outweighed by the gains from belonging to a healthy, stable macroeconomic area

Finally, it can be argued that the exchange rate is not the optimal instrument for adjusting to asymmetric shocks. In fact, unless accompanied by appropriate domestic demand and supply-side policies, variations in the exchange rate can be expected to have only transitory effects upon the real economic variables.[10] In the final analysis the development of an area depends on productivity growth, which in turn is linked to the size and quality of investment (in physical capital, in technology, and in education), and to the presence of entrepreneurial spirit and efficient public administration.[11]

The experience of southern Italy illustrates this clearly. Since the Second World War, the period in which the north-south gap was narrowed was when the Bretton Woods system of fixed exchange rates prevailed. During these years, the Government's efforts to promote southern development were stronger and above all more efficient. More recently, the depreciation of the lira since 1992 does not appear to have brought any appreciable advantage to the Mezzogiorno, which exports only 7% of its output, compared with about 25% for the northern part of the country.

In a word, I do not believe that it is possible to draw incontrovertible conclusions concerning the impact of EMU and the introduction of the single currency on the development of the less prosperous regions.[12] The policies adopted at national and European Union level will be crucial. This is clear to the national governments, and it is clear also to the Commission, which in recent years, first with the Edinburgh initiative for growth and then with its White Paper, has sought to be a catalyst, mobilising private as well as public resources and capital to create jobs and improve the Union's infrastructure.[13]

---

[10] De Grauwe, P. (1994), *The Economics of Monetary Integration*, second revised edition, Oxford University Press.

[11] In a recent study Putnam (op.cit) has investigated the links between the shortcomings of 'civic culture' and of 'social capital' in the Mezzogiorno and the region's economic backwardness.

[12] Gros, D. (1996), *Towards Economic and Monetary Union: Problems and Prospects*, CEPS working paper No. 65

[13] Masera, R. (1995), *Per lo sviluppo delle aree depresse: dall' intervento straordinario all' intervento ordinario*, Futura 2000 Editrice.

Conclusion

I have tried in this paper to argue not only that the Treaty of Maastricht and the full realisation of Economic and Monetary Union need not exacerbate existing regional disparities within Member States, but that it may actually permit the pursuit of appropriate policies to reduce these disparities and enhance the cohesion of the Union. The prerequisite for this is the full application of the Treaty, founded on the cornerstone of the stability and budgetary discipline embodied in the convergence criteria, and on economic and social cohesion, as provided for by Title XIV, and in particular Article 130a.

As the decision on the transition to the third stage of EMU and introduction of the single currency approaches, the debate on individual members' compliance with the convergence conditions inevitably intertwines with that on the appropriateness and correct interpretation of the criteria themselves.[14]

The criteria were designed to enable the monetary union to be constructed under conditions of stability and budgetary discipline. These goals cannot but be endorsed, for they assure an environment conducive to the expansion of output and employment and to increased welfare. For that matter, the criteria contained more wisdom than they are credited with by those who only see them as a set of numbers that have transformed the construction of EMU from an historic economic and political decision into an exercise in arithmetic.

The criteria laid down by the Treaty for the size of the government deficit and public debt and the complicated 'excessive deficit' procedure represent a compromise between those who consider that within a monetary union the budgetary discipline must be regulated by rigid rules and those who feel that union is compatible with reliance on fiscal co-ordination governed by suitably flexible procedures.[15]

The question is significant in the context of the European Union's regional policies. Because the EU budget will remain a tiny fraction in comparison with national budgets for the foreseeable future, Union fiscal policy will amount to the policies pursued by the Member States.

[14]   Kenen, P. (1992) op. cit.; De Grauwe, P. (1994) op. cit.; Savona, P. (1995), *L'Europa dai piedi d'argilla*, Libri Scheiwiller, Milan.; European Monetary Institute (1995), *Progress Towards Convergence*, Frankfurt.; Gros, D. (1996) op. cit.

[15]   Padoa-Schioppa, T. (1994) op. cit.; Allsop, C., G. Davies and D. Vines (1995). *Regional Macroeconomic Policy, Fiscal Federalism and European Integration,* Oxford Review of Economic Policy, Vol. 11, No. 2.

If the latter are held in a straitjacket, the Union as a whole will be incapable of responding to shocks that particularly effect certain regions. On the other hand, rules that are too lax, or the absence of rules altogether, would raise the risk of 'free riding', possibly tempting member countries into undisciplined fiscal policies in the hope of shifting the inflationary cost to the entire Union.

A comprehensive reading of the Treaty of Maastricht makes clear its high political purpose of union, cohesion and progress for Europe. It is the achievement of these aims that provides the motivation and justification for the commitment of individual governments to economic convergence; for convergence should not be seen as an end in itself, but as the condition that makes cohesion and progress possible.

When fiscal issues are dealt with by an Italian, his listeners may be inclined to suspect that he is trying to justify his country's past fiscal prodigality, and perhaps prepare a rationalisation for future prodigality. This is not my position and certainly not the position of the Bank of Italy. Although the ratio of the budget deficit to GDP is still high, it improved by a full two percentage points in 1995, the first improvement for 15 years; and if one excludes the high interest charges on the national debt, there is now a primary budget surplus, amounting to 3.5% of GDP. The adjustment to public finances now underway in Italy must proceed without pause, and the Bank of Italy's rigorous monetary policy will aim to bring down inflation so that it comes into line with that of the most virtuous member countries.

With the restoration of financial balance in its public accounts and the eradication of inflationary expectations, Italy can look forward to lower long-term interest rates (during the past two years the differential between our ten year Treasury bonds and equivalent Bunds has varied from 4 to 6 percentage points). The government budget will then become once again an effective tool of economic policy.[16]

These are prerequisites also for effective policies for the depressed areas. More substantial public resources can then be available to complement those provided by the Community Structural Funds; and indirectly the depressed areas will benefit from faster growth for the entire national economy made possible by a lasting financial equilibrium.

[16] I agree with the view expressed in Gavin McCrone's paper for this Colloquium that nation states should retain enough fiscal headroom to run their own countercyclical policies.

The present debate on compliance with the Maastricht criteria and on the costs and benefits of the EMU echoes that conducted in Italy forty years ago, on the eve of the initial creation of the Common Market itself. In his memoirs, Guido Carli, the former Governor of Bank of Italy and Minister of the Treasury at the time of the Maastricht negotiations, recalls 'the fears and mental reservations present within the country' with regard to the Treaty of Rome, and how a top industrialist was 'terrified at the idea of the progressive dismantling of tariff barriers'.[17] After nearly half a century, there is simply no denying that the nation's participation in the European Community has favoured both its economic growth and its civic progress. It is hard to tell in advance how a society may respond to decisions of historic scope; nor would it be appropriate to do so by a simple extrapolation from past experience, which by definition cannot include a decision to break with that past. Theoretical models can help identify the weak points that future policy will have to address. But the future is no deterministic sequel to the present. The future has to be constructed.

[17] Carli, G. (1993), *Cinquant' anni di vita Italiana,* Editori Laterza, pp. 164–65.

Discussion following Carlo Santini's paper

At the start of the discussion, it was suggested that Dr Santini's argument that EMU carried no threats for the regions was at variance with the points he himself had made about the scale of the regional problem in Italy, and with the need, despite very large amounts of expenditure over many years, for the south to receive continuing financial support. Perhaps Italy itself was not truly an 'optimum currency area', and the trade and budgetary deficits in the south referred to by Dr Santini would have caused the Mezzogiorno to devalue if it had had a separate currency. Such action would make its economy more competitive.

While lower inflation and lower real interest rates could be beneficial to all areas if these followed as a consequence of monetary union, these effects could be completely counterbalanced by relative movements in real earnings. The monetary union between East and West Germany provided some salutary lessons. The rise in East German wages in an effort to achieve comparability with the West had worsed the competitive position of the economy of the former East Germany; and it was partly as a consequence that the drop in output there following unification was even greater than had taken place in other eastern European countries since the collapse of communism.

Although there was research to show that the core countries of Europe (France, Germany, Benelux, Denmark and Austria) were less likely to suffer from asymmetric shocks than the United States, this was not true of the European Union as a whole. The Atlantic countries (Britain and Ireland) and the Mediterranean countries (Portugal, Spain, Italy and Greece) were likely to be quite differently affected by the economic cycle and by external events.

A recent article by Sir Martin Jacomb was referred to as contradicting Dr Santini's view that monetary union would not aggravate the regional problem.[1] This argued that economic forces, left to themselves, would always tend towards the concentration of activity in geographical centres, and that Government intervention was necessary, through the operation of regional policy and automatic fiscal transfers, to disperse it so as to ensure that less fortunate areas could also benefit. While this was admitted to be an extreme statement of the contrary point of view, it was argued that Dr Santini had not given adequate

[1]   *Sunday Telegraph,* 24 March 1996.

recognition to the dangers which monetary union would pose to Europe's poorer areas, particularly in the light of the very limited resources and powers available to the European Union.

A number of speakers claimed that the results of regional policy had been disappointing in some parts of Europe, not only the Mezzogiorno. But this view was strongly challenged, and reference was made to the considerable progress made in Ireland, Spain and Portugal as a result of support from the European Structural Funds. It was also pointed out that Scotland itself had received considerable benefit from the Structural Funds, particularly in the development of essential infra-structure which had helped the growth of the economy.

Dr Santini in summing up said that the problem of the south of Italy was not simply an economic problem. In his view the economic aspects were less important than cultural factors, lack of education and long-held traditions. It could therefore not be solved solely or even mainly by economic means. It was for that reason that he did not fear the effect of the European single currency upon it: a single currency might not help it, but he did not believe that the problem of the Mezzogiorno would be exacerbated. Nor did he accept, apart from any political considerations, that it would be in any way assisted by separate curren-cies, a southern lira and a northern lira, within Italy.

He did accept that EMU involved risks, especially in the transition to a single currency. But essentially it was a political choice and, in his view, it would not work without the support of public opinion. This was a far more important condition of success than being able to meet the technical requirements of 3% budget deficits and 60% debt levels.

Several speakers had referred to the importance of labour mobility. Labour mobility from the south of Italy to the North and to other parts of Europe had been very important between 1945 and the mid-1960s; at that time it had helped to reduce the excess amount of labour in agriculture. It was less important now and the opportunity for it was also less. But mobility of capital, which could take place more easily within the Single Market, especially after EMU, could also be impor-tant in helping the less developed parts of Europe.

So far as regional policy was concerned, experience in Italy showed that its effectiveness depended much more on the way it was applied than on the amount of money spent. Furthermore regional growth would remain disappointing unless infrastructure was sensibly planned and provided to give maximum economic benefit, and unless traditions and culture were changed. Above all investment would not take place unless those responsible had confidence in the rule of law and the stability and reliability of the political system.

IX Concluding Remarks

Gavin McCrone

Norbert Walter began his paper by describing how his feelings as a German, and in particular his country's experience of two world wars, had provided the mainspring for his commitment to European integration. It was the same political commitment among the six founder countries in the 1950s that led to the Treaties of Paris and Rome and the type of European Union that we now have. The Union has never been a purely economic or free trading arrangement; there has always been a political objective, even if, as Bruce Millan said, the extent and shape of future political integration remains undefined. Recognition of this is of central importance in explaining the difference in attitude towards EMU between Britain and her partners. It is partly because the political objective of the European Union has never been sufficiently widely understood in Britain and, where it was understood, not shared by large numbers of people, that EMU has received the reaction that it has.

Despite a heavy reliance on international trade, Britain remains a rather isolationist country. And it still sometimes seems to have difficulty in deciding whether to commit itself wholeheartedly to Europe or to cultivate some alternative Atlantic arrangement. As a leader in *Le Monde* very rightly said of the British '*ils doivent choisir leur continent*'. But in my view our country has no realistic alternative to Europe, either economically or politically, however much people may like to think so – certainly not one that would give it the kind of influence it can have in the European Union. If that lesson remains to be learnt, part of the reason may lie in history: the inadequacies of the nation state having been less forcibly demonstrated to Britain than to other European countries. EMU has brought this difference in perception between Britain and most of her Continental partners about the objectives of the European Union into the open so that it can be fudged no longer.

EMU could still be derailed if some event in France or Germany, the two major states that are essential for it to start, prevents either of them from joining in 1999. But many of those who have spoken at this Colloquium have increased my belief that it will go ahead, and go ahead approximately on time. It needs to be recognised that the effort and cost of preparing for it are so great, to say nothing of economic sacrifices in trying to meet the convergence criteria, that the more time elapses, the more aborting so great an enterprise will become unthinkable. As Norbert Walter said, if it does not go ahead, it would not be possible to mount all this effort again within a generation. There is, therefore, a determination in Europe to achieve it, despite the difficulties; and, at least until recently, this commitment has been seriously underestimated in Britain.

Does the Single Market Need a Single Currency?

A number of those who spoke drew attention to a difference of emphasis between my paper and Bruce Millan's on the need for the Single Market to have a single currency. He points out that, since Member States all signed the Single European Act in 1986 and have now implemented the Single Market in advance of monetary union, EMU cannot be essential to it. He accepts, however, that currency stability is necessary to make the Single Market work.

It is also widely said that many British industrialists who strongly favour the Single Market remain unconvinced of the need for EMU. But the businessmen to ask about EMU are not the British or Italians, who have benefited from currency depreciation, but their counterparts in other countries which have not devalued. Since 1992 there has been widespread concern in France and Germany that competition from Britain and Italy was unfair because of currency depreciation. Whether those depreciations truly reflect economic fundamentals or amount to beggar-my-neighbour policies would be hard to prove one way or the other. But what matters is how they are perceived. Beggar-my-neighbour policies only work if neighbours are prepared to be beggared. And as soon as industrialists become widely convinced that competition is unfair, Governments would come under severe pressure to introduce some kind of trade restriction, regardless of any treaty obligation they may have. If the Single Market is to be opened up as intended, therefore, and is to last without countries seeking new ways to protect their industries, there must be confidence that exchange rates properly reflect the competitive strength of national economies.

In the past the ERM was able to provide a substantial measure of currency stability. It did not bring all the benefits that might be looked for from a *successful* single currency, but neither did it carry the risks, since exchange rate adjustment, usually with agreement, remained as a measure of last resort. But although the ERM system worked well in the 1980s, and its success made possible the introduction of the Single Market, it broke down in the early 1990s, partly because of the strains resulting from German unification, but also partly because of the lifting of exchange controls. The easier capital movements become, the more difficult it is for governments to defend the value of their currencies against international speculation. At the meeting of finance ministers in Verona in April 1996, it was proposed that, in order to prevent disorderly exchange rate movements giving rise to unfair competition, a mark III-type ERM should be created for countries that will not be ready to participate in EMU at the start. But if it involves a return to narrow bands for the member currencies, it is likely to be subject to the same kind of pressures as undermined the old ERM in 1992 and 1993; and if the fluctuation bands remain as wide as they are at present, this hardly gives the degree of currency stability that is required.

The Regional Issues

There are two aspects to the regional issues. The first is the economic balance between Member States after EMU, which, as Bruce Millan rightly said, would become increasingly like regions in the single European economy. The second is the problem of the existing disadvantaged areas, such as the Mezzogiorno of Italy (about which Carlo Santini spoke), parts of Ireland, Spain and Portugal, and of course the less prosperous regions in all of the countries, including Britain.

(a) Balance between Member States

As regards the balance between the economies of Member States, I remain of the view that the key requirement is to be able to keep inflation rates broadly in step. A single monetary policy will admittedly make it easier to achieve this; but it is far from guaranteed if account is taken of the very different attitudes and labour market institutions in the Member States. If, after joining EMU, rates of inflation remain significantly different for tradable goods and services, the countries with higher inflation will suffer rising unemployment and stagnation. In the end that stagnation will probably control the inflation, but at a cost that is likely to be politically unacceptable. The result could therefore be a breakdown in EMU, with one or more countries finding themselves forced to secede. Not only is convergence in rates of inflation therefore, in my opinion, the most important of the convergence criteria, but the formal requirement – a rate of inflation not more than 1.5% above that of the three best performing countries – may not be strong enough. Not only does the criterion say nothing about the levels of unemployment that might accompany such an inflation rate, but if, as at present, the annual rate in the three best performing countries is about 1.5%, Britain would still qualify with an inflation rate twice as high. That would soon lead to a loss of competitive position and stagnation.

My reservations on the fiscal criteria, as explained in my paper, are of the opposite kind: that they are too tight and inflexible. There is something wrong with deficit and debt criteria that few of the candidate countries are able to meet. Without doubt Germany, Austria and the Netherlands could go ahead with monetary union tomorrow without the least anxiety, because they have shown that they have been able to maintain their currency parities in relation to each other for more than ten years. Yet neither Austria nor the Netherlands meet the fiscal criteria at present. Nor does Germany, and recent economic forecasts suggest that Germany may have difficulty in meeting both the budget deficit and debt targets targets by 1998. That Germany should not qualify is obviously absurd, when it is Germany's example of monetary stability that everyone else is trying to emulate. But if, as is sometimes suggested, the criteria were adopted to keep out weaker economies that might threaten the success of EMU, stretching them for Germany, and enabling France to meet them only by clever bookkeeping, will make it difficult to avoid stretching for other countries too.

Obviously fiscal prudence is essential if EMU is to succeed, just as it is a condition for currency stability in a national economy. But the 3% deficit criterion, if strictly adhered to, could impose a straitjacket that makes it very difficult to operate an effective counter-cyclical fiscal policy or to take appropriate action to deal with external asymmetric shocks. The result could therefore be serious economic imbalances between countries.

It is evident that if the economy of a particular country is suffering, for whatever reason, the problem areas within that country will suffer along with the rest of the country; and they may suffer disproportionately, just because they are the weaker parts of that country's economy. But the appropriate action depends on the origin of the problem. If it arises through persistent failure to achieve convergence of national inflation rates, it is useless to try to tackle it by fiscal transfers either to a region or to the country as a whole. Larger and larger transfers would be required and the cause of the problem would remain unresolved.

But if it is due to an external asymmetric shock, including an economic cycle that is out of phase with that of other countries or a greater sensitivity to some external event, it would be best dealt with in the first instance by giving national fiscal policy sufficient headroom to stabilise the economy. And if it is so severe that it would in the past have been handled partly by exchange rate adjustment, some form of fiscal transfer within the European Union in support of the country may be necessary. Transfers on the scale originally envisaged by the MacDougall committee, to which a number of speakers referred, are not thought to be necessary, for the reasons explained in my paper, and they are certainly politically impractical.[1] But some mechanism is certainly required if the risks of external shocks are to be contained, and it is regrettable that no scheme has so far been put forward, even along the lines of the more modest proposals in the report of the Reichenbach group.[2]

It may well be that the absence of such an arrangement could at some early stage precipitate a crisis in EMU.

(b) The Disadvantaged Regions

It was argued in the discussion following Carlo Santini's paper that the situation of the presently disadvantaged regions could indeed be made worse by EMU. Perhaps I went too far in my paper in discounting this. I fully accept that the Single Market required regional policy to be strengthened. Without it the benefits of fuller integration, rather than being shared, might accrue to the stronger and most advanced regions at the expense of the weaker. What the monetary union will do is make

[1] CEC (1971), *Report of the Study Group on the Role of Public Finance in European Integration* (MacDougall Report), Brussels
[2] CEC (1993), *Stable Money: Sound Finance*, (Report of the Reichenbach Group), published in *European Economy,* No 53, Brussels.

the Single Market more complete: to that extent, some further strengthening of regional policy may be called for, and the Structural Funds were, of course, further increased following the Maastricht Treaty. But in other respects I do not think it will make very much difference to the regional problem, and I therefore agree with Bruce Millan when he said that if EMU is good for a country, it will be good for the regions of that country. Indeed it is possible that the greater ease with which capital will be able to flow across national boundaries, in the absence of exchange risk, will make it easier to develop those parts of Europe where labour is plentiful and cheap. What will happen, I expect, is that some of the regions will do better and some will do worse, depending on how well they can take advantage of opportunities in the Single Market and how successfully they can attract investment funds. Success will depend not only on economic factors but, as Carlo Santini said, on whether the area is attractive, on the quality of infrastructure, on stability in politics and on security in law and order.

Some speakers, including Norbert Walter, suggested that, because the regional problem was a consequence of the operation of the market, intervention was neither appropriate nor likely to be effective. But the experience of the Scottish economy since the war, and its remarkable transformation from the older industries of steel, shipbuilding and heavy engineering to lighter industries and services, is a clear refutation of the view that regional policy is ineffective. It is because of that policy that Scotland is now a major centre for the electronics industry. That does not mean that Scotland is a poor location, or that the industry would do better elsewhere. The purpose of regional policy is not so much to subsidise areas as to enable them to realise their potential, so that they can contribute to the rest of the country and to the European Union, instead of having to be supported with unemployment benefit and social security. Regional policy should be seen not as charity but as an investment to increase future prosperity.

Various people mentioned migration. As I pointed out in my paper, one of the differences between the United States and Europe is the greater acceptance in America of massive population movement. For linguistic and cultural reasons, population movement between the countries of Europe can never be expected to come near to the flows of population between individual states of the United States. Nor would it be sensible for Europe to aim to achieve that. But with low population mobility, capital mobility to less prosperous areas becomes all the more important, if underused labour resources are to be brought into use.

That will, of course, depend on costs remaining attractive, particularly in relation to productivity. But flows of capital to the poorer areas can be expected to occur more easily when exchange risk is eliminated; and it is one of the main purposes of regional policy to assist that process.

Britain and EMU

Monetary union is sometimes represented as yet another example of Britain missing an opportunity to play a constructive part in a new European initiative, with the probable result that it will eventually have to join a scheme that has been devised to suit the needs of others. But it would not be right, just because of past mistakes, to force the pace on something so important and so risky as monetary union. It would be irresponsible to join without a careful assessment of whether Britain can meet the conditions to make membership a success.

On the economic front, although the rate of inflation is better than it has been for many years, it is still significantly above that of Germany and France. Against the D-mark sterling has steadily depreciated, so that it is now only worth half its 1981 D-mark value and a quarter of its 1965 value. Britain still has to prove that it can do without the twin drugs of inflation and depreciation; and until that can be demonstrated, joining EMU would be a risky venture. There is also cause for concern over the apparently different timing of the economic cycle in Britain and in Continental countries and the much higher volume of short-term personal debt, which means that the British economy would react more strongly to movements in interest rates. That is why my paper argued for a period in which Britain could show that it could maintain a steady value for sterling against the Euro, rather as the florin and the schilling have successfully shadowed the D-mark and the French franc, despite periodic attacks, has managed for ten years to maintain its central D-mark parity within the ERM.

Britain is equally unprepared politically. The Government has not put to the people the positive case for EMU, or even, in recent years, for European integration. The Eurosceptics have been allowed to make the running; and what the people have heard from the Government have been repeated doubts and reservations about a range of European initiatives, and in particular about EMU. It is scarcely surprising in these circumstances, therefore, if the British population as a whole remains unconvinced of the merits of EMU membership. Yet for an undertaking of such importance and involving substantial risk, a Government must be assured of strong public support. Without it, the first time unemployment rose or a recession occurred, it would come under strong pressure from the large body of Eurosceptics in Parliament and in the country who would seek to blame the crisis on monetary union and would argue strongly for Britain to leave. But to join and then leave again a few years later would be to repeat the ERM fiasco on a bigger scale and with much graver consequences. Not only would the damage to Britain's economy be severe, but the cause of European integration would also receive a major setback. Indeed it is possible that if Britain left EMU after joining, the political pressures would result in it leaving the European Union altogether, or at least being relegated to a peripheral role.

The right course, in my opinion, is therefore for EMU to go ahead with the six or eight countries that feel confident they can make it work and have demonstrated that they can match the German and French inflation performance. That would exclude the four Mediterranean countries, at least in the first wave. Britain likewise, given its economic record and its political unpreparedness, is an improbable candidate for joining in 1999. It would be better, in my view, to accept now that early British membership is unrealistic, but to stop playing the awkward squad by raising objections to almost every initiative that other Member States bring forward, in particular over EMU, thereby losing influence and goodwill. Britain should make it clear that it recognises the advantages of EMU and intends to join when it is felt that the economy has achieved sufficient real convergence and harmony of operation with the other economies of Europe to be confident of making it a success. In the meantime there is a major and rather neglected task to be tackled: to establish a workable relationship between the Euro and the currencies of those countries that will not be in EMU at the start, so as to ensure the monetary stability that is essential for the maintenance and successful operation of the Single Market.